Hidden Genius
Frank Mann, the Black Engineer Behind Howard Hughes

by H. T. Bryer

D1518935

Grey Forest Press

Oak Harbor, Ohio

Hidden Genius: Frank Mann,
the Black Engineer Behind Howard Hughes

Copyright © 2011 by H. T. Bryer

All rights reserved. No part of this book may be reproduced or
transmitted in any form or by any means without written permission of
the author.

Published by

Grey Forest Press, LLC
PO Box 225
Oak Harbor, OH 43449

www.GreyForestPress.com

Design by www.CompassRose.com

ISBN 9780983258308

LCCN 2011924036

Categories:

1. Biographies-ethnic-African-American
2. History-American-African American
3. History-American- African-American-Military Aviation
4. History-American-Automobile design
5. History American-Aerospace

"The greatest pleasure in life is doing what people say you cannot do."

—*Walter Bagehot, British essayist and journalist 1826–1877*

Acknowledgments

Foremost, I would like to thank my brother and collaborator Paul Bryer, without whose prodigious memory and tenacity this story would have died out, faded, and passed with the memories of those who knew Frank and knew of his incomprehensible accomplishments and contributions to the world.

The particulars of these historic events and Frank's associations with the twentieth century's greatest scientists, aviators, and movie stars were recorded by Paul on video and audio tape and taken down in mental notes and filed away neatly in his memory. As I wrote this story and tried to arrange it in an orderly fashion, if I found myself getting stumped or if I lost my place and I needed some mental traction to continue my forward motion in the storyline, all I had to do was call my brother Paul, ask him a few questions about certain events or situations, and those distant worlds, be it his and Frank's of the disco eighties, or the simple times of Frank's childhood, nearly a century ago, would flood back in crystal clarity, as if Paul had taken a trip in a time machine and was actually there with Frank Mann and Howard Hughes when they lived this history.

I can't forget my brother, Michael Bryer, whose undying enthusiasm and efforts to lend a hand to this endeavor has led us down some very interesting avenues. I'd also like to thank my editor, Joanne Asala, for all of her helpful suggestions.

And I'd be remiss not to thank my beautiful wife, my sweet mother, my two lovely daughters, and my darling granddaughter, Sissy, for just being.

Table of Contents

Preface

Frank Calvin Mann (December 19, 1908–November 30, 1992) was a mechanical genius. He was an aeronautical and aerospace engineer, award-winning sports car designer, soldier of fortune in the Second Italo-Ethiopian War, primary civilian instructor of the famous Tuskegee Airmen, and a World War II officer in the Army Air Corps. Another interesting fact about Frank—he was a lifelong friend and associate of, and behind-the-scenes troubleshooter and engineer for, the world-famous film producer, industrialist, philanthropist, and aviator, Howard Hughes—who at the time was one of the richest men in the world.

Frank Mann owed his education and career to Howard Hughes, and he repaid his friend and mentor Howard by remaining loyal to him into his twilight years. Whenever interviewers asked him questions about various covert Hughes projects, Frank would often say, "Howard's men don't talk." And when asked about Hughes's eccentricities and racial prejudices, Frank always defended Hughes.

"Howard had his hands in a whole lot of things. He didn't have time to waste on people who were not involved. If you worked with Howard and got to know him, you would find that he was a fine person and you would easily accept him as a brother."

Frank's story is one of the great-untold stories of human accomplishment. His remarkable story would have largely gone unknown were it not for several momentous events.

First, like his lifelong friend and mentor Howard Hughes, Frank suffered a break-in at his place of business. It was not a covert operation, like the 1974 burglary at Hughes's headquarters on Romaine Street in Los Angeles, the results of which sent shockwaves through the intelligence community when a stash of Howard Hughes's secret memos came to light. Frank's break-in happened at his humble south Houston auto repair shop one night while he was out nightclubbing. He didn't lose any secret documents, but the burglar had gained access to the cash that Frank kept in his shop apartment by cutting a hole in his roof. When Frank discovered rain pouring in, he realized he needed someone to fix it. Enter my brother, Paul, who happened to be the person that Frank's property manager, Harry

Richeck, called to do the job.

When Paul was called out to repair the roof of Frank's shop, it was the very first time that he ever laid eyes on Frank; he recalled that Frank was dressed in an old dark-blue jumpsuit and he was wearing an old pair of loose-fitting leather shoes with no socks.

"He was sitting on an old fold-up chair in front of his garage. His hair was all messed up and he was swatting at flies with a flyswatter. My first impression of Frank was that he was a bum."

After a short introduction, Frank led Paul into his shop where Paul looked up and assessed the damage—a broken fiberglass skylight panel in the metal roof over Frank's shop office.

Paul went right to work replacing the skylight and sealing it in. After he loaded his tools, he went back into Frank's shop to wash his hands. Frank handed him a white towel and asked, "Young man, how much do I owe you for your work?"

Paul answered, "You don't owe me a thing, sir; I did this job as a favor for my friend, Mr. Richeck."

"Well, you are not my friend, and I really do appreciate what you have done for me. I have to pay you something. How about a history lesson?"

Paul smiled at Frank. "Sure, history was my favorite subject in school."

Frank took Paul into his office, which doubled as his living quarters. As Paul entered, he looked around to see that the walls were covered with framed historical photographs of airplanes and sports cars. Several large auto show trophies sat on a shelf in the corner.

"Hey, sir," Paul commented, "this looks more like a museum than an auto repair shop office."

"You're right; it is a museum, and you are looking at the biggest artifact in here."

"What do you mean by that, sir?"

"Call me Frank and be frank with me. When you first saw me, what did you think of me?"

"Well, I just thought that you were a worker here."

"Come on, Paul, be honest. What were you really thinking?"

"To be perfectly honest with you, sir, the way that you were dressed and wearing those old shoes and having your hair messed up like that, I thought that you were a bum."

"Fair enough. Now, Paul, would you like to know what my first impression of you was?"

Paul answered, "Shoot."

Frank Mann

"When I saw you drive up here in that fancy pickup truck with chrome wheels, and I watched you strut up here in pressed jeans and two-hundred-dollar cowboy boots, like you owned the place, I said to myself, 'Frank, that boy ain't no roofer.' But you proved me wrong, Paul. Now it's my turn to prove to you that looks can be deceiving."

Paul looked Frank in the face. "Listen, Frank, you don't have to prove nothin' to me. I can tell by the way that you conversate, that you and me can see eye to eye. Now, what about that history lesson?"

Paul looked around again at the office where he stood, which was a literal museum of Frank's extraordinary life and remarkable accomplishments. Frank gave Paul a personal tour that impressed the younger man so much that he added a new goal to his life. This new goal was to let the world know that one of the world's greatest aeronautical, aerospace, and automobile design engineers was alive and well and living in a little apartment inside an auto repair shop in a rundown section of Houston. And that he was Black.

Chapter 1
Frank Mann &
Howard Hughes

Frank Mann had the deck stacked against him from the very start. A Black child born to an unwed mother in 1908 Texas didn't have much hope of becoming a success in life. In his own words: "What was there for me to look forward to but the things Black people could do in those days, like being a shoeshine boy, a porter, or a cook?"

When Frank was six years old, his pretty mother, Ina Beatrice Hill—who had now become a schoolteacher—did something that would change his life forever. She got married to a man named Lewis Jackson Mann. Frank now had to compete with a grown man for the attention and affection of his mother.

"It made a man out of me fast," Frank would later relate. "My stepfather was very jealous of the close bond that my mother and I had, and he was very critical of me."

Even at this young age, Frank had his own personality and mature grasp of right and wrong.

"When I was nine years old, I looked at my mother and father and I said that when I grew up, I wasn't going to be like them. They were uppity; they had no time for the average person on the street. Unless that person had something important to say to them, they figured that the average Joe had no business talking to them. Because they were educated and school teachers, they thought that they were better than the man on the street. I made up my mind that I was going to accomplish great things in my life, and no matter how big I got, I would always treat the other guy the way I would like to be treated."

The first time that Frank saw an airplane up close was when he was nine years old and living in Dayton, Texas, just northeast of Houston. "It was a World War One biplane that had run out of gas and landed in a field near our house."

Frank was so impressed that he began building small model airplanes out of bits of wood, cardboard, and paper. His stepfather must have thought Frank a good craftsman, because he displayed the model airplanes that Frank built in his classroom for his students to see.

As Frank grew, he developed a love of mechanical things. By the time he was eleven years old, he was nearly six feet tall and he spent as much time as he could repairing cars for his neighbors. This new hobby was driving Frank's parents crazy. They both wanted Frank to become an educator, like themselves. The thought of Frank growing up to be a common grease monkey didn't sit well with them, but Frank was obstinate about his new vocation.

Frank's mechanical activities outside of his home, which happened to be one of the more well-appointed two-storey brick houses on Wheeler Street, drew the attention of a notorious local gambler and entrepreneur, Don Robey—the Don Robey, who later became the famous, and according to some, infamous Black record producer, talent manager, and song writer.

Don had an eye for business opportunities and he quickly made a deal with this young mechanical whiz kid. He would supply the customers and buy the auto parts, and Frank would do the repairs.

Frank was doing well as a partner in the shade tree mechanic business. He had made enough money to buy his own car, and he had fallen in love with a thirteen-year-old girl he had met in school.

Frank was on top of his world when, one day, he saw his partner—a grown man—kissing his girlfriend. Frank became so upset that he thought about killing himself. With tears streaming down his face, he got into his car and he started driving aimlessly. He could hardly see the road. He swerved and narrowly missed a large tree. He wanted to end it all but he just didn't have the guts.

As he neared the south side of Houston, he came upon an airport and he saw a sign that said: "Airplane rides, one dollar." He had that dollar in his pocket and he made up his mind then and there that he was going to pay the dollar, get way up in the sky, and jump out of the airplane and kill himself. However, as that growling biplane thrust Frank into the air, it was so exhilarating that Frank forgot all about his cheating girlfriend. "Forget about girls; this is for me."

He had lost one love and gained another, and this new one was really exciting.

From that day on, Frank spent every day he could hanging around the airport. He observed the mechanics and pestered them until they let him repair torn fabric on the airplanes and do mechanical work on the engines.

From left to right: Unidentified person, Frank Mann, Howard Hughes.
In an airfield south of Houston in the 1920s.

"I wasn't getting paid, but I was learning."

There was another boy who frequented this particular airport. He had been watching Frank and wondered why in the hell all of these pilots were letting this lanky Black kid work on their airplanes. As Frank tells it, "You see, at that time, Black people didn't have anything to do with airplanes."

This other boy who was so curious about Frank would later become his best friend and together their designs and inventions would help revolutionize the world. This boy's name was Howard Robard Hughes and this airport just happened to be near his father, Howard Hughes, Sr.'s, tool company and the place where they kept their airplanes.

One day, young Howard approached Frank and introduced himself. The two young men got to talking and Howard told Frank that he was having trouble with his biplane. It seemed that every time Howard would let go of the stick, the plane would either climb or dive, a common problem in those early days of aviation. Frank agreed to try to solve the problem for Howard. So they set up a meeting at Howard's father's shop on Polk Avenue at seven the next morning.

That night, Frank was so excited that he could hardly sleep. He arrived early at the Hughes Tool Company and he had walked into a production area to look at the materials at hand. "I walked in and I thought that I had the run of the place, because young Howard was there."

One of the shop foremen saw Frank nosing around. He grabbed him by the arm and called him some nasty racial epithets. As he was roughly escorting Frank to the door, young Howard Hughes burst in on the scene. "What do you think you're doing?"

The foreman answered, "This nigger was messing around with the tools in here."

Howard ordered him to let go of Frank. "From now on, you are to address this person only as Mr. Mann, and you are to assist him with anything he wants to do in this shop."

"Yes, sir," said the bewildered foreman, and Frank went to work building the parts he needed to fix Howard's airplane.

Frank solved Howard's level flight problem. According to Frank, "The solution was an early form of autopilot." From this first project, a friendship began that lasted for more than half a century.

Throughout his career, Howard Hughes depended on Frank to help him solve problems that his White engineers couldn't. According to Frank, "Every time that I came up with a solution to one of Howard's problems, he would pat me on the back and say, 'I didn't think it was in you, but you've got it!'"

Frank's interest in airplanes blossomed in high school. Howard Hughes financed Frank's building of a low-wing monoplane while he was attending Houston's Wheatley High School. Frank built the airplane in a garage owned by a local detective friend. To test his new airplane, Frank took it out on the street and taxied it up and down until a policeman stopped him and ordered him to, "Get that damn thing off of the street!"

When Frank finally decided that his creation was airworthy, he took off near the high school. He circled the school several times and then he crash-landed in a pasture. A local radio announcer reported the crash and Frank's stepfather picked up on it right away. He rushed to the scene and promptly gave this budding young aviator a whipping he never forgot.

Howard and Frank had a lot in common; they were both only children and they both had doting mothers. Howard's father's business ventures kept him away from home and distant, while Frank's stepfather was by nature distant and critical. The boys also both shared a love of aviation and mechanical things.

Howard made his own battery-powered bicycle when his mother would not allow him to buy a motorcycle. He would ride it all over his neighborhood and charge kids a nickel to ride on it. When he was fourteen years old, he showed up at a local auto dealership and, after inspecting a Stutz Bearcat sports car, he wrote down his name and address on a piece of paper and ordered the dealer to deliver the car to his home. The incredulous dealer called Howard's father to tell on his loony son. To his surprise, Howard Senior told the dealer, "Give the boy whatever he wants; I'll pay for it."

When Howard got the car, he drove it around for a few days and, to the astonishment of his father, he completely disassembled it and then put it back together.

Frank and Howard spent many hours together working on various projects. Because the White engineers refused to work with a Black man, Howard often would dismiss them and bring Frank in. Sometimes he would smuggle Frank in, in the back of a panel truck or hidden underneath blankets, so that the jealous White engineers wouldn't see him.

Whenever one of these long engineering sessions ended, Frank would go quietly back to his abode or a nearby hotel room, where shortly thereafter one of Hughes's assistants would deliver to him a small manila envelope stuffed with cash. Howard's White engineers would then be called back to the project and, to their astonishment, the amazing Howard Hughes had "solved" all of the design problems.

Howard and Frank both loved to read newspaper comic strips. Howard would bring a collection of these clippings into their engineering sessions, so that they could read them to each other on their breaks. According to Frank, he would play Mutt and Howard would play Jeff, of the famous *Mutt and Jeff* comic strip. Frank even had a small tattoo of Mutt on one of his arms and a tattoo of Jeff on the other.

For nourishment, Frank said that they would bring in ham sandwiches and drink bottles of beer from Howard's father's brewery. For dessert, they would eat Baby Ruth candy bars.

Chapter 2
High School
& College Years

In his high school years at Phillis Wheatley, Frank got a lot of help from his teachers. His auto mechanics and science teachers went out of their way to help this bright student. They sometimes even helped him after school on his various projects.

Frank continued to repair cars all through his high school years, and he used the money that he made to help pay his expenses in college. At the behest of his parents, Frank enrolled in Prairie View A&M, an historically Black college in a small agricultural community about fifty miles northwest of Houston.

At college, Frank continued to make money fixing cars for everyone from the college president to the faculty.

While at Prairie View, Frank built one of his first custom cars. "People would stop to ask me if it was a car or an airplane on wheels, because it had no steering wheel. It was steered by a joystick. It was painted silver and it had airplane fins. Several times, I drove it to Beaumont to visit a girlfriend. It was the fastest thing on the highway. I even had to slow it down to let the highway patrolmen catch me. They were so amused by this unusual car that they never gave me a ticket. Some of them even asked me if they could take it for a spin. I got so tired of being stopped by the police and curious onlookers that I eventually got rid of it."

At the end of his first year at Prairie View, Frank concluded that he couldn't learn any more there than he already knew. Frank didn't want to go there in the first place. His parents had twisted his arm to attend because it was their old alma mater. However, he also didn't relish the idea of breaking the news to them, so he tried to soften the blow with a little characteristic humor. He asked his parents if they wanted him to learn to put "sparkplugs in watermelons," because Prairie View College was an agricultural and mechanical school, situated in a region of Texas that was well known for its watermelon production.

Now that Frank had given up on Prairie View, he set his sights on a college that could teach him both aeronautical and automotive engineering. His only problem now was to find one that would accept a Black student. Frank finally picked the University of Minnesota, where he majored in science and studied aerodynamics.

At the University of Minnesota, Frank was both enjoying himself and working to the best of his ability to outperform his white classmates. He knew his work was superior, but one of his professors gave him a B, instead of an A. Frank brought it to the attention of the professor, who agreed with Frank's assessment.

"Frank, the reason that I am twice as stringent on grading you as the others is because you are Black and you will have to be twice as good at what you do in order for you to compete and succeed in life."

Frank also attended Ohio State University. Two weeks before finishing school at Ohio State, he was called into the office of one of his favorite professors.

"Well, Mann, I bet you wondered why I called you into my office. I bet that you thought that I was prejudiced and I didn't like you. Well, I do like you. But I saw the makings of a good man if I stayed on your back and was hard on you. Now, I want you to remember this when you go out into the world. Don't use the old cliché 'because I'm Black, they won't use me.' The white man will use you if you can make him some money, and when you don't make him money, he will fire you. You are going to file a lot of applications that will end up in the wastebasket, but somebody is going to accept you, and then you will be able to write the size of the check that you desire."

After graduation, Frank went to Compton, California, where he got a job with Sundstrand Corporation building aircraft components. After a year of employment with Sundstrand, Frank left and began work as an independent engineer.

In 1934, Frank learned that Howard Hughes was in California and he contacted him. Howard invited Frank to a meeting and gave him a job as an aeronautical engineer for his newly formed Hughes Aircraft Company. Hughes Aircraft, a division of the Hughes Tool company, would later become famous for the Hughes H-4 Hercules "Spruce Goose," among other projects.

In the years that followed, Frank worked as an independent engineer for such companies as Lockheed, Boeing, and other California aircraft manufacturers.

Spruce Goose. Image courtesy US government.

"I never got on anyone's payroll," Frank said. "I mostly worked on design plans for aircraft, and I redesigned components to make certain that the aircraft would work properly."

Chapter 3
Paul, Frank &
Errol Flynn

My brother Paul was the sixth child born in our family of six boys and three girls. He was always a curious kid and he spent a lot of time hanging with my paternal grandfather, Harry, who was always around us. Grandpa Harry and Paul were buddies.

Grandpa loved to tell us stories of the good-old days when his family worked the Great Plains seasonal wheat harvest from Oklahoma to Canada. They were horse traders and they supplied large teams of horses needed to pull the gangplows and wheat reapers. Grandpa was born at the end of one of these seasonal runs in Winnipeg, Canada, in 1885. He spent most of his life traveling and he had lots of stories to tell us. My brothers and I would often spend part of our summer days sitting on the green grass under a shade tree, listening to Grandpa tell us stories of his adventures. As he talked, he would take a swig from his pint bottle of whiskey or take a swallow from his cold bottle of Falstaff beer.

One of his more memorable stories was about the time when his car broke down in the 1930s, and the famous bank robbers Bonnie and Clyde gave him a lift to Stillwater, Oklahoma. It seems Bonnie needed a match to light her cigarette, so they stopped and picked Grandpa up. He sat in the front seat beside Bonnie; Clyde was driving. He lit her cigarette and she offered him a drink of whiskey from a flask. Grandpa took a swig and thanked her kindly. The two men in the back seat didn't talk much. Grandpa thought it was funny for them to be wearing overcoats on such a hot day, and the overcoats didn't do much to cover their Thompson submachine guns, anyway.

Grandpa requested to be dropped off just outside of town so he wouldn't get any bullet holes in him. They complied with his request, and Bonnie thanked him for the box of matches that he gave her.

Another story Grandpa told us was about the time that he and his younger brother Ollie were almost abducted by body snatchers in Kansas

City, Missouri, just before the turn of the century. The body snatchers favored kidnapping and murdering transient people to sell to medical schools for dissection, as their disappearances wouldn't cause much of a stir in the local community. The story went, as the boys were walking home from a tent show one evening, they were stealthily approached from behind by two men in a rubber-tired buggy pulled by a horse with rubber booties. The driver asked the boys where they lived. Grandpa had the presence of mind to tell him that he lived in the mansion that they were standing in front of; it happened to be a local doctor's house. The men drove on and left them alone.

As my brother Paul grew up, he yearned to hang out with his older brothers. By the time Paul was sixteen years old, he was going out to dance clubs with us. Paul was a forward character, and like Frank Mann, he never met a stranger. I remember one night when four of us brothers were at a dance. We were standing around like bumps on a log for an hour or so. It was a place we never had been before, in a new town, and we were too backward to just go up and ask a strange girl to dance. So we settled for watching everyone else while they danced and had fun. We were sure surprised when Paul approached us with three pretty girls in tow. He smiled and, one by one, grabbed each of our hands and placed one of the girl's hands in each of ours and said, "There you go, boys, now go and have some fun."

When Grandpa died of cancer in 1975, Paul really took it hard. After all, he had lost his best friend, and I think that's why, when Paul met Frank, he instantly took to him. After a few visits, Paul opened up to Frank. "You know, Frank, I had a grandfather whom I was very close to; he died about four years ago and I still miss him. But you know, you kind of remind me of him."

"That's a funny thing, Paul, because I had some dear friends that I was also very close to, Howard Hughes, Humphrey Bogart, and Errol Flynn, and do you know, you remind me of them, especially Errol. He was quite a ladies' man. You know Howard taught me to use my mind and engineering skills, but Errol taught me how to be a ladies' man."

Paul is always ready with a quip or joke. Sometimes, when he meets a stranger, he'll shake their hand and initiate a conversation by saying, "Shake the hand that shook the hand of the man who shocked the world." Naturally, the person whom Paul was addressing would want to know what Paul was talking about, so Paul would tell them that he had been privileged to have shaken Muhammad Ali's hand and that he had also shaken hands with

Elvis Presley.

Paul is proud to be a Texan and sometimes, after being introduced to a person, he will announce to them in his Texas drawl, "I wasn't born, bred, and raised in Texas, I was *bred*, born, and raised in Texas."

Frank had a very similar sense of humor and easy way with people. One of Frank's come-on lines when he met a woman was, "Pardon me, I'm a stranger in town, could you please show me the way to your house?" This line almost always got a laugh and set the mood for friendly conversation.

When Frank lived in Los Angeles, he would often join his friend Groucho Marx at a table in the Brown Derby restaurant. Frank was one of the few people who could trade jokes with Groucho and hold his own ground. Frank claimed that Groucho's famous bigamy joke from *Animal Crackers* was originally his:

Capt. Spaulding (Groucho Marx): [to Mrs. Rittenhouse and Mrs. Whitehead] Let's get married.

Mrs. Whitehead: All of us?

Capt. Spaulding: All of us.

Mrs. Whitehead: Why, that's bigamy.

Capt. Spaulding: Yes, and it's big of me, too.

Errol Flynn was one of Frank's close friends, whom he liked to talk a lot about. Back in the forties, one of these two Romeos had a legal problem and was accompanying the other to court for moral support. During a break in the court proceedings, they went up on the rooftop of the court building to relax and have a smoke.

While they were chatting, Errol produced a handful of golf balls from his pocket. It seems he had been on the golf course just before he came to court. To Frank's amazement, Errol Flynn began throwing the golf balls from their lofty perch to the street below. The white projectiles struck the hard street and they bounced amazingly high. Several hit cars and continued bouncing on down the street. Frank was shocked. "What are you doing, man? You are going to cause damage with those balls!" Errol calmly answered, "Settle down, Frank. I'm just trying to give you a little business. That is your auto body repair shop at the end of the street, isn't it?"

Frank was involved in showbiz himself. He claimed to have been on the set and to have done stunt pilot work for Howard Hughes in his 1930 epic film about WWI aviation, *Hell's Angels*. He assisted Howard on other movie projects, and around that time he played both principal roles on a production of the popular, though controversial, comedy radio show *Amos 'n' Andy*.

Frank gave Eddie "Rochester" Anderson, comedian Jack Benny's sidekick, flying lessons, and their mutual love of sports cars kept them in contact for years. Frank was also a friend of Herb Jeffries, "The Bronze Buckaroo," the first Black singing cowboy. Jeffrey, who also sang with Duke Ellington's band, was featured along with Eddie Anderson and Frank in an April 1954 *Ebony Magazine* article about Frank's award winning sports car designs entitled "Sports Car Builder."

Among the Hollywood celebrities Frank built custom sports cars for was Mickey Rooney, Walt Disney animator Bill Justice, and orchestra leader David Rose, famous composer of the instrumental piece "The Stripper."

Another good friend of Frank's was the famous baseball pitcher Leroy "Satchel" Paige. Frank traveled for a while on a bus tour with Satchel and

Negro Baseball League legend Satchel Paige (left) partying with Frank Mann (center) and friends at the Eldorado Ballroom, 1942.

his Negro league team, the Kansas City Monarchs. Satchel visited Frank in Houston in the early forties and they partied together at the Eldorado Ballroom.

Chapter 4
Joined at the Hip

B ack in the early eighties, when Paul first told me about his new friend Frank, I really didn't know what to think. "Harry, you have got to meet this old Black guy; he's something else. He's a real comical character; he lives in a little apartment that he built in the corner of his auto repair shop—and he was Howard Hughes's friend."

Right off the bat, I wasn't very impressed. I couldn't see why Paul would be so excited about knowing an auto mechanic, even if he had been acquainted with Howard Hughes. "Okay, Paul, when I get down to Houston, we'll have to go over and pay him a visit."

*Frank Mann (left) and Paul Bryer (right) with Bill Bush,
Howard Hughes's chief pilot for thirty-four years.*

When I got down to Houston that fall, Paul took me over to Frank's place, which was situated in an older, run-down industrial part of Houston, not too far from downtown. We cruised up to a complex of four attached metal buildings. Frank's auto repair shop was in one of these units. Frank greeted us cordially as we entered the large open garage door. After a little small talk, Frank gave me the grand tour, starting with his prized hand-built miniature live steam locomotive, the Santa Fe Texan. It's about ten feet long and weighs a ton and a half. He built it from scratch to prove that he knew something about steam engines, when the all-White Live Steamer Club of Los Angeles snubbed him when he tried to join their organization in the late sixties.

We proceeded into his apartment, where he showed me all of his historical photographs, awards, and memorabilia. Now I understood what all the fuss was about. I was standing in the presence of, and engaged in conversation with, a man who had worked with some of the greatest scientists, aerospace and automotive engineers, aviators, and celebrities of the twentieth century. And Frank did it all against the odds. His color never deterred him. He never settled for where society wanted to place him. Frank's attitude was, "If I can accomplish what the average wouldn't even consider, then I knew that I would be accepted for what I could do and not for what I am."

I got to know Frank in those first few days that I was around him. Paul and I accompanied Frank to local Black nightspots. I got to see firsthand and appreciate the greatness of Frank's personality and his love for his fellow man. When Frank entered a bar, all of the attention was on him. His friends and the club owners would raise a ruckus and beg Frank to get up and show off his dancing skills. Or the band would stop playing until Frank would get up on the stage and sing the blues or launch into one of his outrageous monologues.

One memorable evening, Paul and I were guests of Frank's at a nearby Black club called The Edge of Night. Frank was invited up on stage, to the delight of the audience. Now Frank's style of comedy is not what you would expect coming from a seventy-eight-year-old comedian. Frank started one of his monologues with, "Folks, I've got the cutest little wife; I'm so proud of her that I wanted to bring her up here tonight to show her off to all of you, but damn it! Her husband done come and got her and took her home."

Next, he introduced the audience to his own version of "Mary Had a Little Lamb." His version went like this: "Mary had a little lamb, its fleece was black as jet. I met a girl in here last night and I ain't stopped scratching yet!" To illustrate his joke, Frank started scratching his thigh.

I thought that this off-color joke at the expense of the clubs' female patrons might draw some anger or insult, but I was wrong. I looked around at the women and they were laughing just as hard as the men were.

Frank added several more comical and racy jokes to his performance. He then walked back through wild applause to our table.

In the early days of Frank and Paul's friendship, when they were just getting to know each other, Paul received a call from Frank inviting him to his birthday party. The party was to be held at a nearby club, Murphy's.

Frank sent a limousine to bring Paul to the party. When Paul arrived, he was escorted in and seated at a large table beside the guest of honor, Frank.

Frank was dressed to the nines, as usual, except this time his chest was covered with fives, tens, and twenty-dollar bills. They were neatly folded and pinned to his lapel as birthday gifts from his friends. The table before them was loaded with a selection of odd dishes, many of which Paul, the only white guest, could not identify. He later learned that the pot with all of the chicken feet sticking out of it was chicken soup. Another pot contained collard greens and hog maws (stomach of a pig), and yet another contained mustard greens and ham hocks.

Paul scanned the table. He then looked at Frank and asked, "Frank, what kind of food is this?"

Frank jokingly answered, "How the hell do I know? Most of my life I ate dinner with millionaires."

They enjoyed their meal and when the party started, Frank was taken aback when Paul was given as much attention from the guests as he himself. When the music started, Frank discovered that Paul was also a worthy adversary on the dance floor.

They enjoyed each other's company, and the fun and entertainment that they had at this party must have proven to each of them that though they were generations apart in ages, and of different races, they were both cut from the same cloth and joined at the hip. From this day until the day that Frank died in 1992, they became a dynamic duo, inseparable friends on a mission to spread the word about Frank's unrecognized accomplishments to schools, the media, Hollywood, or to anybody who would listen—and to have as much fun as they could while they were doing it.

Chapter 5

Ethiopia, Tuskegee &
the "Spruce Goose"

One evening, Paul invited Frank over to have dinner with his family. Paul had introduced his wife Debbie to Frank and he had brought his young daughter Azur and son Adam over to Frank's shop on several visits. Frank took to them; he even allowed young Adam to ring the bell on his model steam train, the *Santa Fe Texan.* If you knew how particular and protective Frank was of this masterpiece of his own creation, you would understand that this was quite a privilege.

After dinner, Paul asked Frank if he was interested in being interviewed about his accomplishments by a reporter from a large Houston newspaper.

"I've been talking to some newspaper people, and they want to do a story on you, Frank. What do you think about it?"

"Bring them by if you think that they are good people. I'll trust your judgment."

"Great, Frank. I'll give you a call and set up a date."

But Paul didn't give Frank a call for several weeks. When he heard from the reporter that she could do the interview the next day, Paul, in his excitement, gave her a tentative okay, and he headed over to Frank's shop.

"Frank, I've got the newspaper interview all set up. The reporter can come over tomorrow. Can you get all duded up and be ready?" Frank was tired; Frank was dirty; and Frank wasn't feeling his best. He threw his hands up and he gave Paul a look that could kill.

"It's off! I am not doing any interview! You can't operate like this with me. You should have notified me and asked before you told anybody to come over here."

"But, Frank, I just heard a short while ago that she had an opening. This is a very busy woman."

"I don't care. It doesn't matter; I'm done. As far as I am concerned, this whole project is done."

Frank walked back into his office. He sat down at his desk and began opening his mail. Paul followed him in.

"I'm sorry, Frank—you're right, I'm wrong. I made a mistake. Everybody makes at least one mistake. Can't you forgive me this one mistake, Frank?"

Frank didn't speak for a short while. He continued opening his mail as if he hadn't heard Paul's apology. He looked up at Paul. "Okay, you admitted you were wrong. I'll let the lady interview me, but not right now. I'm going to have a party at a club next week; you can invite her to the party. After that, we can come back here for the interview."

When the date arrived, Paul met the reporter at the club. Accompanying Paul was our younger brother, Robert, and our actor friend, James Drury. They were very excited about getting to meet Frank. Frank was prepared. He was dressed in a dapper suit and was wearing his best hat.

The party was a smashing success. At the party, there was a soul band. Frank sang with the band, he performed on the dance floor, and everybody had a good time.

After the party, they all convened at Frank's shop.

After a brief warm-up tour, Frank agreed to let the reporter take a few snapshots of him. "You look great, Mr. Mann, and one of these pictures will make a great cover shot."

The reporter asked and was given permission to photograph the historical framed photographs, awards, and memorabilia that decorated Frank's office.

With Frank as a guide, the newspaper reporter began to photograph Frank's prized memorabilia. The reporter pointed to a picture on the wall showing a handsome twenty-something Frank standing beside a sleek racing monoplane.

"Mr. Mann, what can you tell me about this picture?"

Frank studied the picture; he then replied, "This plane, at the time, was one of the fastest airplanes in the world. Against the orders of the U.S. government, I crated this plane up in the mid nineteen thirties and shipped it to Ethiopia, by way of Canada. I was planning to fly reconnaissance for the Emperor Haile Selassie, during the Italo-Ethiopian War."

The reporter said, "Now that's very interesting, but why did you have to ship out from Canada?"

Frank answered, "I had heard a lot of talk from other Black aviators about our Ethiopian brothers in Africa. And at the start of the war, they only had a few airplanes and pilots to protect them against the might of the fascist Italian army. So I felt obliged to do my part for my African brothers.

Frank Mann in Canada, circa 1937.

"I had planned to embark from New York, but the F.B.I. stopped me and threatened to arrest me if I tried to take the airplane out of the country. So I flew the airplane to Canada. I disassembled it, crated it, and I had no problem shipping it from there."

By now, the reporter was all ears. "How interesting. Do you mind if I turn my tape recorder on?"

Frank said, "No, go right ahead." And he continued with his tale.

"I was only in Ethiopia for a short while before I had a big confrontation with the emperor himself."

The reporter adjusted her recording gear, listening intently as Frank continued his story. "I had flown several missions. One day, I had engine trouble and I didn't show up as an observer on the battle line. So the emperor sent a captain to see what was wrong. I returned with him to the palace, where the emperor questioned me. 'Why didn't you fly your mission?'

"I told him that I had problems with my airplane and that I was trying to repair it before I took off into the air again.

Frank alongside the Wedell Williams 92.

"Haile Selassie got very angry and he said, 'Don't you know how to notify people?'

"I said that I was sorry, but then he did something that made me angry. He called me 'an American black nigger dog.' I couldn't take that, so I told him, 'Your highness, you need me, I don't need you.' So then I left."

"How did you get away, Mr. Mann?"

"I just grabbed my suitcase. I threw it into the cockpit of the airplane, and I took off for Europe."

"I bet they didn't like that."

"What were they to do? They sure couldn't catch me. When I got to Europe, I joined a flying circus. I was a wing walker, a parachutist, and a daredevil stunt pilot. In Europe, very few people had ever seen a Black pilot, so I drew a lot of attention. I was even entertained several different times by royalty. I did that for a while. Then, I decided to come back home."

The reporter then asked, "Did you return to Houston?"

Frank answered, "No, I couldn't stand for that. You see, at this point, I had tasted respect, accomplishment, and the better things in life. It was out of the question for me to go back to Houston, where a Black man couldn't even drink out of the same water fountain as a White man. So I returned to California, where the sun shines on both sides of the street."

The reporter turned off her recorder. "You must have gotten out of Europe right before the Nazis invaded Poland."

"Yes, I did. Shortly after that, I arrived in America. I was contacted by the U.S. government and asked to train Black pilots at the Tuskegee Institute. Due to the pressure exerted by civil rights organizations and the Black press, in 1939 the U.S. government sponsored African-American flight training with the Civilian Pilot Training (CPT) Act. The Act authorized selected schools to offer primary flight training for pilots, in case of a national emergency. Schools for African-American candidates included Howard University, Tuskegee Institute, Hampton Institute, and the Coffey School of Aeronautics in Chicago. The government paid for the instruction. Tuskegee Institute originally offered elementary or primary CPT courses. In July 1940, the Civil Aviation Authority authorized Tuskegee Institute to provide advanced courses in flight training."

Frank (just right of center) in a group of 24 Tuskegee Primary Civilian Instructors.
Courtesy U.S. Air Force Historical Agency.

The reporter made a few notes in her notebook. "What was it like there?"

"Very disorganized and messy, but I loved the party life there. But it didn't take me long to become disillusioned with the program. Those old World War One biplane 'crates' that the government had supplied just weren't airworthy. I spoke with Howard and he made arrangements to have an advanced trainer sent in. But by then, it was too late for me. I had gotten into a whole lot of trouble for partying with the Black officers' wives and White officers' wives around Tuskegee. So Howard pulled some strings and got me out of there before I became the first-ever Black man to be lynched by a bi-racial mob."

The reporter and Paul laughed. When they settled down, the interview continued. "Mr. Mann, what did you do after that?"

"After Tuskegee, I went back to Houston, where I discovered a lively music scene going on. So I jumped right in and got myself involved at the Eldorado Ballroom on Dowling Street. It was the only elite colored ballroom in this part of the country. People called it the Savoy of the south. I not only became the chief MC, there, but I became a big band promoter and booked some of the hottest bands of the period. I booked groups like Arnett Cobb, The Jacket Brothers, and Ike Smalley. Most of your great bands have played there at one time or another. It was the place to be back in the forties and fifties."

Frank told the reporter that around this time, he ran into his old nemesis, Don Robey. Robey had opened a nightclub in Los Angeles and later he came back to Houston and got himself involved in the Houston music scene. Frank explained that, despite the problems that he had with Robey in the past, he actually did a little MC and promotional work for him. But the association didn't last long. Frank complained, "That guy was always trying to throw a wrench into my business plans."

Ironically, Don Robey was much more famous than Frank. His participation was seminal in the Black music industry. He opened the Bronze Peacock restaurant and nightclub, which competed with the Eldorado Ballroom. And later, he converted his club into a record company. He managed and recorded records for some of the most famous Black singers of that era, like blues singer Clarence "Gatemouth" Brown, and Big Mama Thornton. Her number one hit, "Hound Dog," was later made famous by Elvis Presley. He also recorded some of Little Richard's first songs and he beat him up badly once because, he said, "Little Richard got sassy."

Robey managed and recorded Johnny Ace, Junior Parker, Bobby Bland,

and Johnny Otis. He co-wrote "Farther Up the Road," which was a hit for Bobby "Blue" Bland and, later, was picked up by Eric Clapton as one of his staples. He also co-wrote Elvis Presley's number one hit, "Pledging My Love."

Frank Mann, Master of Ceremonies, at the Eldorado Ballroom, circa 1942.

The reporter wrote down a few notes in her tablet; she then looked up at Frank.

"This is truly amazing, Mr. Mann—not trying to get you off the subject of entertainment, but before this interview ends and you shoo me out the door, I really would like to hear about your work with Mr. Hughes on the 'Spruce Goose' [Hughes H-4 Hercules]."

"Honey, you don't have to worry about that. I have shooed a few reporters away, but that was because they asked all the wrong questions, and none of them were as pretty as you."

"Well, thank you, how sweet of you to say that."

Frank liked her answer and he continued with his stories.

"When I got back to California, Howard had this idea about building the world's largest airplane. He brought me the blueprints and he asked me about my ideas on solving some of the problems he had been having. I worked them out, they were used, and it made him appreciate me all the more."

"Did you and Howard work together solving these problems?"

"Sometimes we did, but you see, the White engineers who worked for Howard didn't want no part of me. Once he brought me into his aircraft company and the White engineers were still there. They looked at me and one asked, 'What is he doing here?' Howard told them, 'He's got ideas.' One of them answered Howard in a cocky manner, 'He's got ideas? Where does he wash dishes at?' So, whenever Howard had a problem, he would send them off and meet me privately and we would work the problems out.

"Now, the whole idea of building this giant aircraft came about because the government needed a large transport plane to carry troops and military equipment to Europe, avoiding the dangers of German warships and submarines lurking in the Atlantic Ocean."

The "Spruce Goose." Image courtesy of the Federal Aviation Administration.

The reporter asked Frank, "Why did they build the airplane out of spruce?"

"Actually, the airplane was mostly made out of another strong and durable wood. The frame and the ribs of the 'Spruce Goose' were made out of birch. The exterior shell of the plane was made of Duramold, a strong, plastic-impregnated plywood that could withstand a lot of stress. Duramold made the aircraft both strong and lightweight for its size. During the war, there was a shortage of metals, and there was no way that the government would allow Howard to use aluminum to experiment with when it was such a strategically important metal during the war. So, Howard chose wood as the building material for his giant flying boat.

"I did an awful lot of work on the hydraulic system, which enabled a pilot to operate the flight controls on this huge aircraft. You see, before the 'Spruce Goose,' all rudders and control surfaces on airplanes were operated by wire controls, which were out of the question on the huge 'Spruce Goose.'

"Howard also had problems with criticism over his government funding. People in the government were raising loud complaints about Howard's funding and massive spending on the project. They said that the *Hercules* would never fly, but Howard said that if he couldn't get it to fly, he would leave the country.

"When the airplane was completed, we took it out into Santa Monica Bay and taxied it around for several hours. We did a couple of three sixties and a couple of one eighties, after which we inspected it. We checked all of the stress points and saw that it was still holding together. So Howard said, 'Here we go, boys.' There were quite a few crewmembers aboard plus some press people. Once we got it out there in the bay, to our astonishment and the astonishment of the world, Howard took it up into the air. I flew third seat observer and I was so busy checking instrumentation that I scarcely realized that we had lifted off. We rose up out of the water and flew at about seventy feet elevation for a mile or so. The big ship landed so smoothly that we didn't exactly know when we were down. Howard had silenced his opponents and proved his point, but after the flight, Howard took us to the side and told us to take the 'Spruce Goose' and do what we could to hangar it. He said that it would never be tested again and that it was 'a flying deathtrap.' And that was that."

"Paul, this is remarkable," the reporter said. "I can't believe that I'm hearing all of these great stories from one person. And Mr. Mann, I want to thank you for inviting me into your office and sharing all of this history with me. I'll do my best to honor you and your achievements in my article."

A few weeks later, Paul arrived with a Sunday edition of the *Houston Chronicle* newspaper. "Good morning, Frank. I have got a surprise for you."

Paul unrolled the paper and pulled the leisure section out. The cover was a full-page article on Frank with a large color picture of Frank and the caption, "MR. MANN, A young Black man's knack for mechanics leads to a 50-year friendship with Howard Hughes and some high-flying designs."

Frank was both happy and excited. "You did it, Paul. Do you realize that this is the first time that a major Houston newspaper has ever devoted a full page to a local Black man?"

Chapter 6
America's First
Black Airline Pilot

T hough history doesn't record it, Frank Mann claimed that he was the first Black pilot to fly passenger planes for a major American airline. Frank was hired as a pilot by Northwest Airways, which later became Northwest Airlines. Accompanying Frank on the flights was America's first Black airline flight attendant. Though we don't have her name, we have a picture of her standing beside her Black airline captain (Frank Mann) in front of a Northwest Airlines DC3 airliner.

Commercial airline pilot Frank Mann on the platform loading baggage.
His stewardess and passengers are in the foreground. Circa 1940.

*America's first Black commercial airline pilot Frank Mann with
America's first Black airline hostess.*

Frank's flight attendant got her job for the simple reason that Frank's
boss didn't want Frank to have any problems that might have developed
from him working in such close relationship and tight quarters with a White
stewardess. According to Frank, his new job as an airline pilot didn't last
very long. "You see, when the passengers found out that a Black man was
flying a plane, they would cancel their flights. So, eventually, that got me out
of that job."

Before Frank left the commercial airline business, he did have one memorable flight. He flew a charter for a group of businessmen who turned
out to be Ku Klux Klansmen.

At first, he didn't draw any suspicion from them as he helped his White
copilot load their luggage, though, as he says, "I didn't like the way they

were disrespecting my little stewardess."

When the plane became airborne and the Klansmen finally realized that their transport was being piloted by a Black man, there was a lot of unrest on the plane. Racial insults and loud threats began to fly from the passengers. When Frank reached his limit of tolerance, he made an announcement. "There is an indication of rough air up ahead. You folks had better all fasten your seatbelts!" Frank turned to his copilot. "Hold on! I'm taking this baby to the envelope."

Frank pulled a few extreme test pilot maneuvers with the big DC3, causing the unruly passengers to hang on for their dear lives and cease their threatening behavior.

Chapter 7

Sports Cars,
Motorcycles & Trains

O ne oppressively hot summer day, Paul decided that it was just too darned foolhardy to put himself or his men on top of an industrial building to do roof repairs. So, since his buddy Frank's shop was nearby, he decided to grab a couple of lunch meals at Popeyes Chicken and pay Frank a visit at his shop.

Frank was happy to see Paul and also appreciative of Paul's thoughtfulness. Popeyes Chicken was one of Frank's favorite foods. Frank welcomed Paul into his little air-conditioned office and went to his compact refrigerator for drinks, as Paul set out the spicy, delicious-smelling chicken, hot biscuits, coleslaw, and little bowls of Cajun red beans and rice. Frank asked Paul if he would like something to drink. "What would you like, Paul, fruit juice or beer?"

"I'll have fruit juice, Frank; I'm allergic to alcohol."

Frank turned to Paul and asked, "You are?"

Paul answered, "Yeah, you know, when I drink alcohol I break out."

With a concerned look on his face, Frank asked, "You do?"

Paul smiled. "Yeah, I break out teeth, doors, and windows."

"You rascal; you're pulling my leg!"

"Frank, I'm just joking. I don't want any fruit juice. Just bring me a beer. What's with the fruit juice, anyway?"

"That's all that I drink, Paul, fruit juice or beer."

"What's wrong with water?"

"Well, if you had been in as many places as I have been in my travels around the world, you wouldn't want anything to do with water. It tasted bad and it was not a safe thing to drink. So I still don't trust it."

Frank handed Paul a bottle of beer, then took his seat at the table across from Paul. He devoured a drumstick, a biscuit, and half of his beans and rice. As he was washing it down with a gulp of Miller Lite, Paul asked him a question. "Well, Frank, what about all these Hollywood movie stars, sports cars, and pretty models you have hanging on the wall?"

"Paul, there's quite a few interesting stories hanging up there, but if you're man enough to ask me about them, then I'll be man enough to tell you about them, no pun intended. Would you like another beer?"

"I'm fine, Frank, go ahead."

Frank continued. "While working for Howard, I was privileged to meet and make friends with some of the Hollywood greats, like I told you earlier—Errol Flynn and Humphrey Bogart, John Barrymore, and lots of other notables. And about my sports cars, Paul, it was in the late forties, being out there in California where your movie stars had all kinds of fancy cars. I went around and I saw a few of these cars that were out of this world. There was something about them that really got me stirred up and enthusiastic. So I bought me some tools, I rented a garage, and I began to haul auto parts and pieces there.

The first car that I built there I called "The Eldorado." I had been a band promoter and MC at the Eldorado Club in Houston. It was the elite Black nightclub in Houston, so I named my custom car after it.

"The Eldorado at that time was different than any other car on the street. I had a chance to sell it to a big car company, and I collected royalties from that company for ten years."

In the previously mentioned April 1954 *Ebony Magazine* article about Frank entitled "Sports Car Designer," they mention a car that Frank built in late 1948. "It could have passed for a Tucker, the controversial car that never reached the market. Mann's car is built from a 1941 Chevrolet body with a souped-up 1948 Cadillac engine and a hydraulic transmission. An unusual car in action, it will not run any slower than 40 miles per hour, and obtains a top speed of 160 miles per hour."

Frank continued. "A little after that, I opened a custom automotive shop in downtown Los Angeles on Cahuenga Drive, right down the road from Howard's Romaine Street offices. In 1949, Bill Justice—a famous animator from Walt Disney studios—approached me with an idea for an American sports car. Mr. Justice is famous for his work on several Disney animated movies, including *Fantasia* and *Bambi*. I looked at his design— actually a cartoon drawing; it's that one that you see up there on the wall. I told him 'no problem.' The little sports car that I built for him was one of the first automobiles to have a fiberglass body, wrap-around windshield, and—as you can see here—it bears a striking resemblance to the 1955 Corvette."

"I can see what you're talking about, Frank, shadowbox sides and all."

Artist's drawing of a fiberglass-bodied sports car Frank built in his custom automotive shop in Los Angeles for Walt Disney animator Bill Justice. Circa 1949.

"Shortly thereafter, I decided to design a sports car of my own. I started from scratch and designed it on the lines of the F-86 Sabre Jet, with aerodynamics built in. You see, I was one of the engineers who worked on the designs of the F-86 Sabre Jet. My 'Baby LeSabre' was finished in 1951, and it won the Los Angeles Motorama in 1953 as the Best Car of the Year. And it was voted 'Best Sports Car of the Year 1953' by *Motor Trend Magazine*.

"When I was building my cars, I would always have people coming in and taking pictures and making drawings."

"Frank, I can see that Harley Earl's Dream Machine, the GM LeSabre concept car, is just a larger version of your design. My God! How could you allow these people to get away with it?"

"Paul, I thought it was an honor to have people come into my shop and draw pictures of my designs. I didn't know what was going on. I was just building and having fun myself."

"Well, Frank, why didn't you take advantage of the situation?"

"I'll tell you why, Paul. You know the Big Three stopped Tucker.[1] I'd

---

[1] Preston Thomas Tucker was a car designer best known for his 1948 Tucker Sedan, an automobile which introduced many features that have since become widely used in today's cars.

just built six of these cars. I sold one to Mickey Rooney, and when they stepped in and stopped me, they gave me royalties for about 10 years on the LeSabre and Eldorado and all these other cars. What was I going to do? They had stopped all these bigger, more powerful people than myself, so I had to stop.

One of Frank's Baby LeSabre sports cars on display
at his custom car shop in Los Angeles, circa 1953.

"Paul, at this point, I realized that I could get my money and laugh all the way to the bank—and do you realize what would have happened in the early fifties if the president of color and design at General Motors had

50

paraded me around to the white public and said, 'This Black man had designed this aerodynamic car.' And all the body surfaces of this car were applied to the whole General Motors line. How many White people do you think would've bought their cars? I just cashed my check. You had to do what you had to do in those days. Otherwise, you'd get in big trouble."

Paul pointed to yet another picture. "I've been wondering about this motorcycle, Frank. It looks to me like the very first chopper ever made."

"Yeah, that was in the forties, too. It was the world's smallest and fastest motorcycle at the time. When I was speed testing it on the Bonneville Salt Flats, it became airborne at 130 miles per hour. I wrecked it twice. The scars that you see on my face and my body came from this motorcycle.

"I had a little Cushman Eagle; it was capable of about 40 miles per hour, at most. I had some big motorcycles that I rode, but they were always getting me down. I decided that I wanted to build one of my own. So, I took this Cushman Eagle. I tore it down. I put a Bonneville Indian motor in it. I rebuilt the pistons and the forks. I put so many rpms in that engine that it got me down three or four times. I decided that I had better leave that motorcycle alone because it was going to kill me. Well, there was this White boy out there in Los Angeles that loved motorcycles. I guess he must have had fifteen of them. He'd buy these fast motorcycles from different guys. He got after me to buy mine, and I told him no, I didn't want to sell it. He kept after me and he offered me a ridiculous price for it. So I sold it to him with a warning: 'This is a killer bike; I can't tell you what to do with something that you own. Keep it for show, but please don't speed test it.' He had it for four days and he took it out and killed himself on it. It's the only project that I wish I never would have started."

Frank sank into a blue mood as he thought back on this sad event. Paul cut the silence. "Ain't no way you could have helped it, Frank. You gave the guy a good warning. If he was such a speed freak, he would have killed himself sooner or later, anyway."

"I guess you're right, Paul. I hope that I'm not keeping you from anything important with all of this gum rattling."

"No, you're not, Frank. I'll have another beer and now that you're on a roll, could you tell me the story behind your steam locomotive? I've often wondered what could have possessed you to build such a complicated piece of machinery."

"Well, then, I'll have another beer, too, and then I'll take you and tell you all about my baby."

*Frank shows off his attractive sports car and his attractive model
at a Los Angeles car show, circa 1953.*

Frank took Paul into the back of his shop and showed him his pride and joy—a one and a half ton, one-eighth scale model of the *Santa Fe Texan* steam locomotive called a 2-10-4, 5001 series. "Paul, I had always loved trains, but I never had one as a child. Out of all the cars, airplanes, and everything that I have built, I consider this my greatest accomplishment."

Frank and friends show off the trophies that his Baby LeSabre sport car(s) garnered at various auto shows. Los Angeles, circa 1953.

Frank ran his hand over the sleek black engine and smiled. "This train is real, down to every little screw and rivet in the original. I put every inch of this together. A lot of people thought that I bought parts to put on here. Everything that you see on this engine was built by my little brown hands. They didn't build one thing for this engine I could buy. It is a real live steam engine and it makes the sounds of the big engine. It will pull one awfully big load. When I built this engine, I built it for a reason. Then I bought a large piece of property in California and I put an entire railroad on my property. And this was for kids to come over on weekends and holidays and what have you. I was glad to give them rides at no charge, because you see, when kids are having fun together, they don't care what color they are. Give a kid a place to play and they won't notice what race or religion you are.

"Now, let me tell you the story of how I came to build this train. I had quite a setup of HO scale (3.5 mm = one foot) trains running around the walls of my Los Angeles car shop, but they were quite small models. One Sunday, I had some people in from New York and they wanted to go into my office and see the trains run. When we got there, I had a little problem, an [electrical] short, and I could not get them to run like I wanted them to. I was angry, so I took a drive down to Griffith Park. When I got down there, they happened to be having a model steam train convention. So I put on the brakes, got up on the fence, and I began watching the trains. I got very enthused over those trains.

Frank gives children free train rides at his home in
Pacoima, California, circa 1969.

So the next Sunday, I went down to the park where they were running the steamers and I tried to buy a small steam locomotive and join the Live

Steamers Club. But they were prejudiced against Black people and they didn't want no part of me. So I made them a challenge. I told them that I was going to build a bigger, better, and more powerful engine than any of them had out there, and do it by myself in six months' time. Well, when word got out, some of the officers of the club looked me up and made me a $15,000 bet that I couldn't do it, and I took him up on it.

"I got the blueprints for the train from the Santa Fe Railroad and I made wooden forms for the parts and had them cast and I machined them. Working sixteen hours a day sometimes, I completed my engine at a cost to me of $80,000, and in less than six months."

"Frank, did you collect on the bet?"

"You bet I did, and it was sweet revenge. You should have seen those White guys' faces when I put my baby through her paces on their tracks. But later, those fellows became good friends of mine. Walt Disney was a member of the Live Steamers and he and I hit it off. He would come over to my house and ride on my train and I would go over to his place and ride on his train. He even gave me a miniature railroad switch to use on my tracks and I treasure it.

"You know, Paul, I have been offered $150,000 for this train and I turned it down. This train means an awful lot to me. And when I die, I want my train to be donated to the Smithsonian Institution, so something of me, that I made with my hands, can be preserved for people to see, and they can say, 'Once upon a time Frank Mann built a train.'"

Paul was moved by Frank's little speech; the wheels got spinning in his head. "Hey, Frank, my brother Harry knows some people who work for the Smithsonian. Maybe I can ask him if we can set up a request to get your train donated while you're still around to enjoy the honor."

"You're right, Paul. That would be much more fun. I like your way of thinking."

Paul contacted me and I, in turn, contacted a friend who was a curator for one of the museum's divisions. He put me in touch with the curator of the institute's transportation department. When told of Frank's accomplishments, he was leery at first. However, interest in acquiring Frank's steam engine gradually developed after several letters, phone calls, and a video tape compilation of Frank's accomplishments were sent over. In a letter to Paul, the curator asked Paul if he would be willing to finance his trip to Houston for a preliminary examination of Frank's locomotive. By now, Paul was nearly broke and struggling to keep up his own expenses. He was highly insulted by what he perceived to be a slap in the face from his own government. Paul immediately called the curator.

"Sir, Frank has been offered $150,000 for his train. He wants to *give* it to you! He doesn't understand why he or I should have to go to expenses in order for you to take it away from him."

The curator answered, "I'm sorry that you feel that way, Mr. Bryer, but with budgetary constraints, my hands are tied." Paul didn't buy it.

"Well, I think I will have to go over your head on this one. Who's your boss?"

"Mr. Bryer, I have no boss. I am the head of my division."

"Oh, yes, you do have a boss and I am going to contact him and straighten this mess out!"

The curator replied, "Please don't do that."

Paul wrote a letter to President George Bush, Sr., who was in office at the time, outlining Frank's accomplishments and his dream of having his masterpiece donated to the Smithsonian Institution. In a short time, Paul received a letter from the president's staff, apologizing about the unfortunate incident and promising their help and support in seeing that Frank got the proper recognition that he deserved. But President Bush left office shortly thereafter, making the promises hollow.[2]

---

[2] When Frank died, the train went to a son (now deceased) who sold it to a past president of the Los Angeles Live Steamers Club.

Chapter 8

Hobo Senior
& Hobo Junior

Frank had two special dogs in his life. First there was Hobo Senior. Hobo Senior was, as Frank liked to call him, "An habitual hitchhiker," because his favorite pastime was to ride on top of the model steam engine coal tender behind his master Frank. He would stand up and bark with excitement as Frank rode his miniature live steam engine, pulling carloads of happy, laughing children around the tracks behind his Pacoima neighborhood home in Los Angeles in the late sixties. Hobo was even featured in a few newspaper articles about Frank and his train, and there is a shot of him standing on the coal tender in a November 1970 *Popular Mechanics* article on Frank's train and railroad. The title of the article was "Sweet Little Santa Fe," referring to Frank's engine, which he named the *Santa Fe Texan*. Hobo Senior also made it to television on an NBC news piece about Frank and his train.

Frank had fond memories of Hobo and, luckily, before he died and broke Frank's heart, Hobo Senior fathered a pup. Frank named his pup Hobo Junior. Hobo Junior was the spitting image of his father and he had the same temperament. As Hobo Junior matured, he and Frank became as close as a man and dog could be. Hobo Junior took his father's place on the coal tender behind Frank. It was as if Hobo Senior had never left. Not only was Hobo Junior privileged to ride on his special spot on Frank's train, but whenever Frank flew to Houston to visit his parents, Hobo Junior was always along for the ride.

Years afterwards, in Houston, Frank was speaking to a group of tourists who had come to his shop on a bus tour. He recounted to them an interesting story about Hobo Junior.

"Hobo Junior used to get in the airplane when I'd fly between Houston and Los Angeles. A lot of times the weather would be bad and I'd put the plane on autopilot. I'd fold my arms and nod off for a while, and do you know that I think? That dog was a former pilot in another life, because if anything went wrong with that airplane, he would wake me up. That dog got so into my life. I loved that dog so much that I could never get another dog. He was with me for seven years and I still dream of that dog. I took him to the vet and he died. I flew him back to California and I cried all the way there. I had him cremated and I threw his ashes into Santa Monica Bay, out at the end of LAX runway where I put his father's ashes, and where I want my ashes to be spread. Maybe me and my dogs will get back together again someday. But I never want to go through losing a dog again and I never want to get married again."

Frank with Hobo Junior.

Chapter 9

Don't Mess with Frank

O ne Thanksgiving, Paul invited Frank to celebrate at our parents' home with our large extended family. Frank was given a seat of honor beside our father, Bud. Frank savored the food and complimented our mother Nell on her cooking. Being polite, Frank ate moderately and didn't ask for seconds. Our slightly overweight father likes to tease people, so when he saw that Frank's plate was empty, he said, "Why don't you push up to the table, Frank, and get some more food, put some meat on your bones."

Frank turned to our father and with feigned indignity he said, "Well, Bud, if I were as big as you, I'd push away from the table. You've got too much meat on your bones."

All eating ceased instantaneously as the room filled with laughter, including Frank and Dad's.

After dinner, Paul drove Frank home and dropped him off at his shop. As Paul was about to leave, Frank stopped him and invited him to his upcoming birthday party. "Paul, next Thursday is my birthday. They are going to have a party for me at The Speak Easy. I'd like for you to come and meet all of my friends."

"Sure, Frank, I'd love to."

"Meet me here next Thursday night at eight."

"Certainly, I'll be there."

Paul arrived on time and parked his pickup. Frank was dressed to the nines and had a limo waiting to take them to the club. Frank ushered Paul into the limo and they left. As the limo pulled out, Frank noticed that Paul was carrying something in a large plastic case. "What you got in there, Paul?"

"It's my video camera. My brothers can't believe all of the stuff I'm telling them about you, so I thought I'd document our escapades for them. You don't mind, do you?"

Frank answered, "No, Paul, I ain't camera shy. You can film me all you want."

The limo stopped outside of the club. The driver opened the door for Frank and Paul and they piled out. Paul turned on his video camera and focused on Frank. Frank gave Paul a proud look as he turned and entered the club.

Frank ran a gauntlet of friendly acquaintances and well-wishers. As Paul made it into the main room, a black hand covered his lens and pushed his camera down. A fugitive from the law, who didn't want his picture taken, confronted Paul.

"Hey, cracker! Don't put that goddamn camera in my face! I'll knock you out if you turn that camera on me again!"

Paul stood his ground. "Hey, Buddy, I got no interest in filming you. What's wrong? You must have something to hide."

That only made the fugitive angrier. "I'm warning you—don't turn that camera on me."

Frank got up in the fugitive's face. "You don't talk to him like that! He can do what the hell he wants to in here. If you don't like it, you can leave!"

The fugitive backed down from Frank, and he faded away into the background.

Frank turned to Paul. "I'm sorry about that, Paul; most everybody who comes in here are good people. I've never seen him in here before."

"You don't have to apologize to me, Frank. Thanks a lot for standing up for me. But I think I could have handled him."

"We came out here for fun, Paul. I can't see you having any problems."

While Paul and Frank were standing at the bar, the MC, Skipper Lee, announced it was Frank's birthday.

"Folks, you all know why we are here tonight. Yeah, we're here to celebrate the birthday of a great Houstonian. And he is a wonderful person on top of that. And here he is, our friend, Mr. Frank Calvin Mann."

The crowd applauded Frank as the band played a short burst of "Happy Birthday." Skipper Lee continued. "Frank, I dedicate your theme song to you and any of the young ladies out there who I know would love to dance with you."

The band began to play the Staple Singers' "Respect Yourself." Two attractive women approached Frank and Paul and led them out onto the dance floor. Frank wowed the crowd with his spectacularly stylish dancing. But soon, Paul was tripping the light fantastic and giving Frank a run for his money.

The fugitive was skulking around the bar, drinking his beer. He had a sour look on his face. He didn't appreciate Frank's popularity with the crowd or the women. His jealousy was boiling over. He cursed Frank under his breath.

The dance was over. The crowd gave the two couples a standing ovation. They walked back to their table. The fugitive watched and moved closer to Frank and his group. The fugitive brazenly came up and leaned down to Frank's dancing partner.

"Hey, girl, how'd you like to dance with a real man?"

She put the interloper in his place. "The only real men that I can see from here are the men sitting at my table."

The fugitive kept on pushing. "What do you want with this old son of a bitch? He can't do you any good."

"Hey, man, why don't you just go away!" she answered.

Frank was burning up. He stood up and in a controlled tone, said, "You heard the young lady. Why don't you leave her alone and just go on about your business?"

The fugitive got up in Frank's face. "You old bastard! You can't tell me what to do. You must think I'm a punk."

Frank was losing his cool. "If you want to keep on using foul language, you and I can step outside where these nice young ladies won't have to hear it."

The fugitive continued with his threats. "Shut your mouth, old man, before I..."

Frank's temper flared. In the wink of an eye, Frank punched the man in the face so hard that he knocked him over backwards. He fell, striking his head against a metal rail support. Frank landed astride him and began mercilessly punching him in the face. Frank delivered several hard blows, then Paul butted in. "Stop, Frank! Don't you think he's had enough? You don't want to kill him, do you?"

Frank stopped. He raised himself off of the man. The man began to moan. Frank looked down at him and delivered a verbal coup de grace. "Respect your elders, punk!"

Several of Frank's friends picked the man up and carried him outside and laid him on the sidewalk. Frank went back to his table. He took a swig of beer. He looked at his bloody knuckles. "Hey, anybody got a napkin? I seem to have gotten a little blood on my knuckles." Paul was dumbfounded. "Man, Frank, I didn't know you had it in you."

A few of Frank's friends were laughing as they approached his table.

One of them shouted, "Hey, Frank! That guy won't be giving you anymore trouble; he's out cold—but don't worry about when he comes to, I'm sure those two nice policemen standing over him will give him a ride."

The women laughed and both of them gave Frank a big hug.

The next morning, Paul drove over to Frank's place to see how he was doing. Frank greeted Paul and showed him the cuts on his knuckles from the one-sided fight. Paul asked Frank, "When was the last time you had a tetanus shot?"

Frank answered, "I'm not concerned."

Paul took some peroxide from a bag and he poured it over Frank's knuckles. As the antiseptic foamed in the open scrapes on Frank's hands, Paul said, "You know, Frank, there are more germs in the human mouth than there are in a cesspool."

With a serious look on his face, Frank questioned Paul. "What are you getting at, Paul? Are you trying to tell me that I am going to die because I punched that fool in the mouth?"

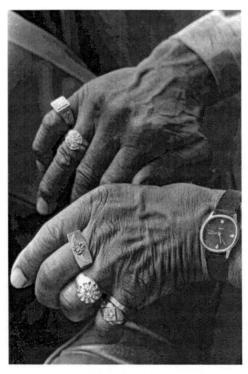

Frank's dukes.

Chapter 10
The Space Shuttle &
Doolittle's Raiders

E very visit Paul had with Frank was a learning experience. Bit by bit, he placed information in his memory about aircraft and other projects that Frank worked on for Howard Hughes. Paul learned that Frank's forte as an aeronautical engineer was his knowledge of designing air surfaces on aircraft. Frank told Paul that he worked on the preliminary designs of the space shuttle to help it glide to Earth without power.

Frank with astronaut Charles F. Bolden, current administrator of NASA.

One day, Paul and Frank were traveling along a highway near a major airport when, to their surprise, a 747 jumbo jet, which happened to be piggybacking the space shuttle, cruised past them at low altitude on the way to a landing. Frank became very excited. "Paul, I built the mechanism that attaches the shuttle to that plane!"

Paul looked at Frank; he was surprised. He had been trying for a long time to get Frank to open up to him about the work that he did for NASA. Frank had always been tightlipped on many subjects unless Paul could first prove that he had some knowledge on the subject himself; this time Frank was different. "You see, Paul, at first they said that the 747 couldn't support the shuttle's weight, but this is a specially reinforced 747. When the plane is flying, the shuttle acts like a second wing, adding lift, like a biplane. So the shuttle doesn't add much weight when they're airborne."

Frank is honored for his work at NASA's Johnson Space Center, Houston.

A few years later, Paul and Frank were invited to a local high school where a group of distinguished Gulf War veterans had been invited to speak. Sometime during the ceremony, Frank was introduced to a decorated 'Top Gun' air force pilot from the conflict. The lieutenant colonel approached Frank, who stood at attention. Simultaneously, they saluted each other. They held their salutes a moment as each man, one in highly decorated military uniform and the other in civilian clothes, waited for the superior officer to release. The officer's eyes were fixed on a large military insignia ring on Frank's index finger. The officer released his salute and Frank followed. "Doolittle?" the officer asked. Frank nodded a "yes." "Doolittle's Raiders?"[3] Frank nodded his head again.

"Oh my God, I am truly honored to be in your presence, sir."

The officer saluted Frank again, this time with much more energy and a loud click of his heels. He spun to the left and marched back to his seat. Paul, who had been standing beside Frank, turned and asked, "Frank, what was that all about?"

A B-25 takes off from the deck of the USS Hornet *as part of Doolittle's Raid, 1942. Image courtesy the National Archives.*

"Paul, I'll tell you later," he replied.

On their way home, Paul learned that Frank met Jimmy Doolittle in the thirties, when he and Howard were modifying a Gee Bee racer for him.

---

[3] The Doolittle Raid on April 18, 1942, was the first U.S. air offense to strike the Japanese Home Islands during World War II. The raid was planned and led by Lieutenant Colonel James "Jimmy" Doolittle (1896 –1993), for which he later earned the Medal of Honor for his valor and leadership as commander of the raid.

Doolittle later set a world speed record with the plane. It was little more than a flying engine, and it had a reputation of killing a high percentage of its pilots. Frank told Paul that later, during the war, he was called upon to assist in preparing Doolittle's B-25 bombers to make them capable of being launched from the deck of an aircraft carrier, enabling Doolittle to bomb Japan early in the war. According to Frank, he was given the insignia ring and accorded honorary membership by Doolittle himself for his contributions to the mission.

Chapter 11

Dinner with the President

During Frank's long career working for Howard Hughes, he helped with designs on the air surfaces and mechanicals of a number of his advanced aircraft. One of these was the H-1 Racer, which broke the world speed record in 1935 by going 352 mph. Its sleek form was said to have influenced the designs of the American P-47 Thunderbolt, the German Focke-Wulf FW 190, and the Japanese Mitsubishi A6M Zero.

Frank also helped prepare Howard Hughes's twin-engine Lockheed Model 14 Lodestar for its record-breaking seven-day flight around the world.

Like the rest of America, Frank was caught up in all of the hoopla of the thirties air races. He traveled to some of these national air races and he had his picture taken standing beside some of the winning airplanes.

Frank said that he once made a special trip to see Amelia Earhart. When Charles Lindbergh became the first pilot to fly non-stop across the Atlantic Ocean in 1927, Frank was so moved that he traveled to New York City to attend his ticker-tape parade.

Frank was also involved in the design and development of the many weapons systems that Howard Hughes produced for the U.S. government.

On the eve of World War II, Frank joined the Army Air Corps. He continued to work closely with Howard Hughes by flying bombers and fighter aircraft to a secret air base near Edmonds, Washington, where he and Howard outfitted the airplanes with Howard's newly developed flexible feed chutes for the onboard fifty-caliber machine guns. Hughes's new equipment increased the rate of fire of the machineguns from fifty to five hundred rounds a minute. A tenfold increase in the aircrafts' firepower, that would help the United States win the war.

After the aircraft were outfitted with the new armament, Frank would fly them to Ellington Field in Houston, Texas. From there, they would either be flown or put on ships for transport to the European warzones.

Frank as an Army Air Corps officer
with an unidentified woman, circa 1942.

After the war, Frank continued to work for Howard, helping him develop other advanced weapons systems. These included wire-guided missiles, radar fire control—which became standard on most fighter jets from the Korean War on—and other advanced weapons systems.

Frank was very tightlipped about these classified projects and before he would discuss them with you, you would have to at least appear to be knowledgeable on the subject or be lucky enough to catch him in good spirits after a few beers.

On one of Paul's informal visits with Frank, while they were talking about Howard Hughes, out of the blue Frank mentioned that he and Howard Hughes had once eaten dinner with President John F. Kennedy. Paul couldn't believe it. "My God, Frank, how come you never mentioned this to me before? What do you remember about it?"

"Well, it was in Los Angeles, and we had filet mignon wrapped in bacon, and it was delicious."

"You ate dinner with the president of the United States and all you can tell me about it was how good it tasted? What did you talk about? Did he say anything of importance to you?"

"Howard did most of the talking, mostly about the space program. But when Howard introduced me to the president, he said, 'Mr. President, this Black man is going to help us beat the Russians in the space race. I think we should let him know that you are going to help his people who are struggling for their freedom.' The president cordially agreed and he shook my hand; it was great.

"So when I wasn't working with Howard on his space projects, he would contract me out to other aerospace companies to work on their projects. Howard would always keep in touch with me to see how things were going. I was his eyes and ears, and I was expected to keep him up on the progress and the competition."

Chapter 12

Shuffle Off to Buffalo

T hrough interviews with an old Hughes Tool Company employee, Paul got in contact with a retired CEO of one of the aerospace companies where Frank had worked. The Hughes employee gave Paul a phone number in Upper Montclair, New Jersey. When Paul called the number, he reached the retired CEO's wife. He told her that he was researching the life story of a Black aerospace engineer named Frank Mann who worked for Howard Hughes, and that her husband's company, Kearfott Guidance Systems, had hired Frank to work on rocket and missile guidance systems.

When the CEO learned from his wife whom Paul was enquiring about, he called Paul back immediately. He told Paul, "Sure, I remember F. C. Mann; he was a likable and very colorful fellow."

Paul told the CEO the story that Frank had told him about his experience going to Buffalo, New York, to work for Kearfott in 1967, during the race riots. Frank said that he had been given a list of special lab wear to purchase and bring to work with him. Because of the riots, the stores and supply companies were either closed or wouldn't let a Black man in. So Frank didn't show up at Kearfott until he was able to procure the necessary lab wear.

He was two days late when he checked in to his new job. His employers were very concerned about his tardiness. The CEO said, "We told F. C. that because he was Black we thought that he may have gotten arrested or caught up in the rioting. Frank didn't like what he was hearing. He told us that he worked for his living, unlike Stokely Carmichael,[4] who was on the dole."

---

[4] Kwame Ture, also known as Stokely Carmichael, was a Black activist active in the Civil Rights Movement. He was a leader of the Student Nonviolent Coordinating Committee and later the Honorary Prime Minister of the Black Panther Party

So Frank went to work and did his job as expected. When Frank learned from management that a congressional oversight committee was coming to tour the facilities and see how their bucks were being spent, he got an idea. The big shots were anxious to see the plant where the future of space exploration was being advanced and they also wanted to see the brilliant Black aerospace engineer whom the plant CEO had been bragging so much about.

When all of the top brass and congressmen were lined up before the large glass window of the hermetically sealed lab room, Frank began his act. Frank was dressed in a sloppy-fitting jumpsuit; his hat was off the side of his head. He entered the room with a large toolbox. Frank took a somewhat impressive-looking component for a missile guidance system and he clamped it into a vice on a table. He then took a two-foot pipe wrench and he attempted to roughly undo some fittings that protruded out of the piece.

Frank acted as if the pipe wrench wouldn't do the job, so he set it down and he started beating on the part with a ball-peen hammer. Frank then opened up a cover and pulled out a handful of wires from the component. He snipped a few wires, stripped the ends bare, then twisted them together and taped them up with electrical tape. Frank studied his handy work for a moment, scratched his head, and then threw the part into a trash can before walking out of the room.

His Stepin Fetchit[5] routine flabbergasted the committee. The CEO told Paul that the big shots were up in arms about the whole thing. "What kind of an operation are you running here? How are we supposed to beat the Russians with this kind of nonsense going on?"

"Luckily," said the CEO, "Frank straightened himself out and came to my rescue. He cleared things up with the committee, explaining that he only wanted to entertain them, and that he had used defective parts in his wacky Vaudeville act."

---

[5] Stepin Fetchit (1902 –1985) was the stage name of comedian and film actor Lincoln Theodore Monroe Andrew Perry. He was the first Black actor to receive a screen credit and the first to become a millionaire.

Chapter 13

Frank Gives Paul the Rights to His Life Story

I n the following years, Paul and Frank continued their visits to schools and organizations, giving inspirational presentations. Paul spent so much time with Frank, researching his career and pursuing various avenues in an effort to publicize Frank's accomplishments, that his home life suffered and his contracting business slipped. Frank thrived on the attention, but Paul's family was beginning to worry about him. Paul had lost many of his industrial contracts and his best employees had left him.

Paul Bryer

One day, Frank called Paul to come over to his shop. When Paul arrived, he was introduced to an attorney. Frank told Paul, "You know, Paul, before I met you, I wasn't doing very well. I didn't feel that I had very much to live for after Howard died. At times, I was depressed and I even had thoughts of suicide. But Paul, being around you made me feel different about my life. It was like being around my old friends Howard Hughes, Errol Flynn, John Barrymore, and Humphrey Bogart all rolled into one.

You have done so much for me that I have decided to give you the rights to my life story. You know, a lot of people have asked me for the rights to my life story, but I refused them. But I know deep in my heart, Paul, that you are the only man that I can trust to tell it the right way."

Paul was deeply moved. "Frank, how did you choose me out of 250 million people to be the one?"

"Paul, I have been around the world many, many times and I chose you out of *six billion* people. When I was a young man like you, Howard Hughes had a lot of confidence in me and he passed the torch to me because of that confidence. I carried that torch all my life, and now I am passing that torch to you, because I have the same confidence in you and I know what you can do."

Frank then signed the papers authorizing Paul to do whatever he wished to do with his life story.

Chapter 14
Paulywood

I t had always been Paul's goal to bring Frank's story to a large audience. He had helped bring recognition to Frank on a local level, but now that Frank had granted him the rights to his life story, he knew that he had the ammunition that he needed to let the whole world know about Frank.

Armed with a film treatment and several story outlines, along with period photographs and video promotional materials, Paul headed off to Hollywood.

Over the years, Paul had been making contacts with people in the television and movie industries. He had friends in the entertainment business in California and Texas. On trips to Hollywood, he had even met with a few old timers who knew Frank in the Hollywood heydays.

Through a phone call to his secretary, Paul contacted producer David L. Wolper and got him interested in the Frank Mann story. Mr. Wolper put Paul in contact with a team of producers who had written and produced some episodes of the blockbuster television mini-series *Roots*, which David L. Wolper had executive produced. These producers were interested in acquiring Frank's story for a high-budget, multi-segment television mini-series.

With help from Paul's old friend James Drury, who starred in the sixties prime time television series *The Virginian*, a meeting was set up between the talent agency that represented Jim and several television production companies.

When Paul arrived in Los Angeles, he met with James Drury at his agency's offices. Before they would represent Paul or the project, he was taken into a boardroom to be interviewed by the heads of the agency. The agency president addressed Paul. "Mr. Bryer, first of all, I would like to tell you that most of the people that we represent here have extensive track records in the industry. Our even considering to represent you is a very unusual event. Don't get me wrong; I understand that you have a great project and you have done a good job of setting it up with some powerful network producers. But before we agree to represent you and your project, we would like to ask you a few questions, just to get to know you and to see if you are the type of person we would like to work with."

Paul answered, "That sounds fair enough to me."

The agency president started. "Okay, you know that we are only going on your recommendation from our client Jim, and we didn't receive a resume from you, so can you tell us about any other projects that you worked on?"

"Well, there's U.S. Steel, Brown and Root, and Waukesha Pierce, for starters."

Frank poses with his four-seat Cessna, Houston, circa 1990.

The agency president interrupted. "I've heard of none of these projects. What was your participation?"

"I guess Jim didn't tell you people much about me, did he?"

The president said, "No, but you can tell us. Were you a producer or director or actor on these projects?" Paul smiled. "I was a contractor."

The agency president looked at Paul questioningly. "What kind of contractor?" Paul quickly replied, "A painting contractor, interior and exterior."

There was an extended outburst of laughter in the boardroom. It got to the point that Paul thought that they were actually laughing at him. "Listen, folks, you may be laughing at me, but I don't see that much difference in what I do for a living and what you people out here in Hollywood do."

The president refuted Paul. "Mr. Bryer, you are so wrong."

"Okay, first I find the project. I contract the project. I direct the project and I complete the project. The only difference between me and you is that if I produce a flop, nobody gets paid." There was yet another outburst of laughter, but this time the agency president was smiling and winking and nodding to his associates. Apparently, Paul had passed their litmus test.

He was told: "Paul, you gave us all the right answers. It'll be a pleasure working with you. Stop by tomorrow afternoon and we will have your contract ready."

Paul came by the following day to sign the agency contract and get the ball rolling. When he signed the contract, he was happy to learn that his new representatives had already set up a seven o'clock dinner appointment at an exclusive Hollywood restaurant for him to meet with the writers and producers of the proposed Frank Mann mini-series.

The meeting went well. They enjoyed their dinner and Paul answered questions about Frank and himself. He explained to them how hard it was for him to pry information about Howard Hughes's classified projects out of Frank. They discussed Frank's Hollywood heydays and his partying with Errol Flynn when he was a member of the rowdy crowd that hung out at Flynn's notorious house on Mulholland Drive.

One of the producers let on that he would like to exploit the angle of Frank as a womanizer. "Man, he was one of the very first Rat Packers. When Sammy Davis, Jr. was still reading comic books, Frank was out there running around with Errol Flynn and Humphrey Bogart. He was partying in all of the Hollywood heyday nightspots, designing futuristic sport cars for the stars, and taking white women to bed. The audiences will absolutely eat this story up."

Paul didn't like what he was hearing. He crushed out his cigarette and he added his two cents to the conversation. "I hope that this mini-series is going to be more about Frank's friendship with Howard Hughes and his many scientific and aeronautical accomplishments."

One of the producers answered, "Don't worry, Paul, I promise you that we will get a good balance of themes in *The Frank Mann Story*."

"I hope so," said Paul. "Frank gave me the rights to his story because he trusted me. I have a responsibility to Frank to see that his story is told with dignity. I don't want anybody to exploit Frank for the sake of sensationalism."

Frank and an attractive young woman at a Hollywood nightspot.

The producers reassured Paul that he has no reason to worry, but this independent stand that Paul took to protect Frank's honor may well have jeopardized the whole project.

One of the producers, whose spirits now seemed a bit subdued, said to Paul, "You will have a lot of input in this project, as you will be working with the writers as a paid consultant. We do need to pick your brain. All of this will be set out in the contract. Our agent will be calling you next week to go over details and set up a meeting."

They parted ways and Paul went back to his hotel to tell his partner, Jim Drury, how the meeting went. The next day, Jim brought Paul over to meet his sons, Christopher and Timothy. Christopher had a music-recording studio, and Timothy played keyboard for Don Henley when he was on concert tour. They met at Chris's studio. Chris had a problem; he was in the process of remodeling his studio to get it ready for an after-Grammy party that he was throwing for his friends in the music industry. He had hired his own drywall men and carpenters, some of whom couldn't speak English. Chris had two days left to finish his project and his prospects of accomplishing this goal didn't look good.

Paul knew that he had some time to kill before his next meeting, so he looked the situation over. He asked Chris what the men's wages were and how much money he had budgeted for the project. With Chris's permission, Paul jumped in and took over. He asked Chris to go to a liquor store and buy several cases of beer and some tequila. Paul talked to the workers. He told them that if they stayed and worked until the job was finished, they would be paid double for their hours worked. He would supply them with all they wanted to drink and he would supply them with meals. They all agreed and went to work with Paul as boss.

Paul went to a grocery store and he shopped for groceries. He prepared meals in the studio kitchen for the men. Paul is an excellent cook and he used his skills to good effect. When the workers got tired, some of them slept on couches in the studio. The morning of the Grammy party, when the Drurys arrived at the studio, they were amazed to find that the remodeling job was completed.

Paul got back to his hotel to get some much-needed rest. He came back to the studio in the afternoon and found that the food and supplies for the party had been delivered. Jim's ex-wife, Tim's mother, was doing her best to try to set up the food and tables with limited help. To her relief, Paul volunteered and went to work setting up the tables, a buffet line, and the decorations. When the guests arrived, Paul pitched in and helped serve the food. After the food was served, Paul took his beer and sat at a table in the corner. He was keeping to himself and enjoyed watching all of the celebrities at the party. As the party began to wind down, Jim came over and told Paul that they had been invited to go with some of their guests to an after-after Grammy party at the famous photographer Francesco Scavullo's gallery.

Paul and Jim arrived at the gallery and they mingled with the guests. Paul looked around for something to drink. There was champagne, wine, mixed drinks, and Perrier, but not a beer in sight. Paul followed some of the waiters as they went to a refrigerator in the back. Mr. Scavullo was standing nearby. "Say, you fellows got any beer in there?"

Mr. Scavullo spoke for the waiters. "No, I'm sorry, we don't."

Jim was right behind Paul. "Paul, you're not supposed to ask the hosts for beer, that's rude."

Mr. Scavullo looked at Paul. "What brand of beer do you drink?"

Paul answered, "Miller Lite."

"Fine, we'll see what we can do." Mr. Scavullo smiled and walked away.

About twenty minutes passed, and Paul and Jim were sitting on a couch when two servants approached. The servants were carrying a large, shiny, galvanized washtub. It was filled to the brim with ice and bottles of Miller Lite beer. Under the direction of Mr. Scavullo, they set the tub on the floor in front of Paul and Jim. Mr. Scavullo smiled and asked, "Will that do?"

Paul smiled back and answered, "I should say so. Thank you very much." Paul reached into the tub and pulled out an ice cold beer.

Jim looked at Paul. "This is embarrassing." Paul took a satisfying drink of his ice cold beer and said, "Partner, never complain about good service."

In the wee hours of the morning, as the party was winding down, Paul and Jim received an invitation to a breakfast party in Malibu. They politely refused the offer, as their meeting with the television producers and agents was scheduled to take place the following afternoon.

The next day, Paul and Jim met at Jim's agency to go over the contracts with Jim's agent. The monetary part of the contract was fair, although when Paul took his share after splitting with Jim, myself, and one other partner, he wouldn't be able to permanently quit his day job. There was a provision to keep Paul on as a paid consultant while the script was being written. But with living expenses in California and a family in Texas, Paul still didn't think he was being compensated fairly for all of the time that he had taken away from his contracting business to research and promote Frank's story. The producers were receiving ten percent of the network production budget. Paul's contract offered him thirteen percent of their part, which was well into six figures.

Paul told the opposing agent that he and his partners needed twenty percent of their budget and some sort of credits, either a "story by" credit or "consulting producer" credit. Through telephone conversations between the agents, the answer came back that their offer of thirteen percent was final, and there would be no credits given Paul or his partners. When Paul heard their answer, he angrily told Jim's agent that "they can stick that contract up their asses." Paul didn't know that Jim's agent had been on his speakerphone with the other agency and that they had heard every word that Paul had said.

Jim's agent called Paul into his office so that he could speak to the other agent on his speakerphone.

Paul told the agent that he could have offered him any percentage but thirteen percent and he would have considered it. "I don't like that unlucky number thirteen, anyway, and I can't understand why you refuse to give us any sort of credit, when it would cost you nothing, and without credits my partners and I will have no hope of continuing doing business out here in

Hollywood."

The agent came back at Paul. "You want control of this multi-million dollar project, don't you?"

"No, I just want to make sure that Frank's story is told for all of the right reasons, so that he can receive the recognition that he deserves for his contributions to the world." The agent had had enough of this upstart Hollywood outsider and he let loose on Paul. "I just can't understand how a person like you can come out here from Texas, barefoot on a watermelon truck, and try to tell us how to run our business. What qualifies you to think that you can mix in our creative and artistic circles?"

"I'll tell you what qualifies me! Frank Mann qualified me! And I don't qualify you! You can take that contract and stick it up your artistic ass! Hey, I think I hear my watermelon truck outside. Have a good day." And that was the end of that.

Chapter 15
The Last of the Hughes Tool Company

It's funny how sometimes things relating to this story work like a Rube Goldberg Gizmo. To illustrate this phenomenon: it was in the late eighties; Frank was sitting outside of his shop one slow summer day. He was watching traffic, the occasional passerby, and swatting the pesky flies that sometimes torment his idle moments. He was approached by a middle-aged Black man who asked him if he wanted to sell him a pile of bricks that were sitting against the wall of one of his unrented shop units. Frank didn't know where they had come from, maybe a former tenant had left them there, but Frank said, "What you want to give me for them?" He sold him the bricks and, as the man was paying him and telling Frank that he was going to use the bricks to build a path in his wife's garden, he noticed that the man was wearing a uniform with a Hughes Tool Company patch on his shirt. Frank asked, "Do you work for Hughes?"

The man answered, "Yes, I do. I'm head of security at the Polk Avenue operation."

Frank answered, "Is that so? Well, you should know about me, then. I'm Frank Mann. I worked for Howard Hughes myself, for more than fifty years."

The man was very surprised. "You've got to be kidding me? I've never heard of you."

Frank put his hand on the man's shoulder. "Well, we've got to do something about that."

Frank took him into his shop and gave him the grand tour. The visitor was amazed and he opened up with some information that he thought Frank might be interested in. "Old Man Hughes would be rolling over in his grave if he knew what was going on with his company. Baker International has bought up the company and they are going to dismantle and piecemeal everything. There will be no more Hughes Tool Company after that." Frank thanked the man for his information; they shook hands and parted.

Frank at the grave of his friend and mentor, Howard Hughes,
Glenwood Cemetery, Houston, Texas.

The next time Frank met Paul, he told him that if he wanted to get any information or pictures from Hughes Tool Company, he had better move fast.

Paul had been calling around, trying to get information about older or retired personnel from Hughes Tool whom he might interview about Frank and his connection to the company. He reached Howard Hughes's cousin, William Lummis, the head of Summa Corporation. Mr. Lummis was receptive and he listened to Paul's story about Frank and Howard. Although he didn't have any information for Paul, he gave Paul the phone numbers of several administrators at Hughes Tool in Houston. Paul called and, to his surprise, he was invited to come and photograph the outside of the buildings.

Paul hired a freelancer who shot news stories around Houston, loaded him and his equipment into his pickup, and went to Hughes Tool. Paul was stopped at the gate by a security guard. When Paul told him what he was going to do, the guard was alarmed and told him that he first had to call his superiors. Paul told him who had given him permission and the guard verified Paul's story. The guard told Paul that he was the first person outside of the company who had ever been allowed to take pictures of the plant. He said that photograph crews from Japan and other countries had tried to do what Paul was doing and all had been turned away.

The guard was Black and Paul remembered the story that Frank had told him about the bricks. Paul asked the guard if he was the one who had bought the bricks from Frank Mann. The guard was very surprised, and he asked Paul, "How did you know that?" Paul went to his briefcase and showed the guard some pictures of Frank and newspaper articles.

The guard said, "So you're the White guy. Frank told me all about you and what you were trying to do for him." He let Paul drive all over the plant with the video cameraman in the back of his truck, filming everything. When Paul was done and about ready to leave, the guard had a surprise for him. "I've talked to my superiors and told them all about you and Frank Mann. They agreed to allow you to go inside Mr. Hughes's office building and film everything, including the company's private museum. They think that it is a good idea to document everything as it is, before it gets dismantled."

Paul and his photographer took their time filming the old photographs, documents, and artifacts. The guard even opened the glass case holding the original model of the Hughes rock-drilling bit and laid the gold-plated device on some black velvet so that Paul could get a better shot of it.

As Paul was getting ready to leave, the security guard told him that there was a basement room under the Hughes offices that contained some precious artifacts that few people knew about and, if he would wait, he would try to get permission for Paul to go downstairs and photograph. Among the artifacts down there, the guard stated, was the Stutz Bearcat sports car that Howard Hughes owned as a boy. It was sitting in a crate. Also down there was a mysterious wooden cane with a goose head for a handle that he referred to as "the Spruce Goose." He said that the cane had belonged to Howard Hughes, Sr. and that Howard, Jr. had taken it on the one and only flight of the *Spruce Goose* in 1947. Howard supposedly used the cane to reach down through an aperture in the deck under his seat to apply pressure to an aileron (wing flap)control that had been causing a problem by sticking. Paul later verified this information with Frank.

Paul waited and was very disappointed when he was refused access to the basement. What became of the purported Stutz and the Spruce Goose cane remains a mystery.

Chapter 16
The Graham Interview

From the filming trip to Hughes Tool and the contacts that he made there, Paul got some information from a man named Tom. "I'm going to put you in contact with Bill Graham. He was the editor of the Hughes Tool newsletter for more than thirty years. He is retired now, but he should be able to tell you something about Frank and Howard."

Paul talked to Mr. Graham several times on the telephone and it was not until February 10, 1993, several months after Frank's death, that he agreed to let Paul interview him.

Paul had Doug Descant, an aviation buff and amateur videographer, set up his equipment in the living room of Mr. Graham's house.

As Doug prepared the lights and tested the audio, Paul talked to Mr. Graham, who was sitting comfortably in his favorite overstuffed recliner with a blanket over his lap. His health was frail and Mrs. Graham stood over his shoulder, making sure that he was comfortable and attending his needs throughout the interview, giving him ice water several times when she thought that his throat might be getting dry from all of his talking. She was a very gracious host and she tried to contribute to the interview whenever she thought that her information might help.

Graham said, "I went to work for Hughes Tool Company in May of 1951. My job at the time was managing editor for *Hughes News*, which put me in a pretty good position to get an overview of the plant operations, and Mr. Hughes himself, except I never met Howard Hughes. Howard, I understand, was in the plant one time during the thirty-four and a half years that I was employed out there.

"About his family, his grandfather Felix was a railroad judge and he was as crooked as a snake. One of the stories I can tell you about Howard Hughes's father, Mr. Hughes, Sr., who had a home on Montrose—or over off of Montrose—he came out one Christmas morning in 1905 and he had a bundle in his arms. He went up to a neighbor lady and said, 'This is what

Santa Claus brought me,' and he presented the world with Howard Hughes, Jr. But there is more to that story."

Mrs. Graham cut in. "There sure was more to that story."

So Mr. Graham continued. "Well, the story that I found out was based mostly on what Bob Moroney told me and what I have since dug up: That Mr. Hughes, Sr. had a girlfriend whom he corresponded with regularly up near Keokuk in Iowa. He would go up there periodically for two or three weeks at a time. Undoubtedly, Howard was a product of that particular union." Mr. Graham paused for a few seconds and looked back at his wife. "I don't know whether I'm getting in over my head here or not?"

Mrs. Graham reassured him. "Well, you're telling the truth, Bill."

"Then what you're saying is that Allene Ganno is not Howard Hughes's real mother?" Paul interjected.

"No, she wasn't, though she was as big an influence on him as a child as anything else. A lot of the things which led to his later being called an eccentric were due in a large manner to the way that he was brought up in the Hughes family. In a household which was a real zoo.

"Howard senior had a brother, whose name was Rupert, a pretty well-known writer at the time. Rupert Hughes had been blackballed in the California film industry for one reason or another and he never got over it. He was quite bitter about it the rest of his life.

"Rupert Hughes had also played a part in the horizontal tunneling machine which Howard Sr. built during the First World War. It was designed to drill from one set of trenches to another with a mine on the end of it which could be detonated manually from the beginning end. It was a mine-laying device. The device was finally turned down by the War Department. In fact, one of the documents that is in the lobby of the Hughes Tool Company is a letter from the secretary of war, saying why the device won't be used. It developed that the warfare at that time had changed from static trench warfare to a more fluid land-warfare operation, with more motorized equipment. The old foot-slogging infantryman was pretty much a thing of the past by the time that the device could have been used."

Paul told Mr. Graham that it was quite an interesting story, but he wanted to get to the point. The whole reason that he had set up the interview was to find someone who could back up Frank's assertion that he was a vital part of the Hughes machine. "Let me ask you this, Mr. Graham. When you were working for Mr. Hughes, did you ever hear of a Black man who was employed personally by Howard?"

"No, I didn't, and I think that was kind of a shame, because Mr.

Hughes, as far as I know, didn't know a White man from a Black man as far as his ability was concerned. He treated us all pretty much the same." Paul showed him a large picture of Howard Hughes's Sikorsky S-43, which was taken in 1991 at Houston's Wolfe Air Park. Standing in the foreground of the picture was Paul, Frank, and several other men. Paul asked Mr. Graham, "Can you identify this airplane?"

"Yes, that's an old Sikorsky. That's an S-43."[6]

Paul pointed to a person in the photograph. "Do you know who this is?" Mrs. Graham told Paul that her husband was blind in one eye. Paul readjusted the picture,

Mr. Graham spoke haltingly. "His name is Ware, I believe."

Paul tried to jog his memory. "Have you ever heard of a gentleman by the name of Frank Mann?"

Without taking his eyes off the picture, Mr. Graham answered very slowly, as old memories flooded back. "Mann is his name."

Paul asked, "Do you know his first initials?"

Instantly, he comes back with, "That would be F. C. Mann."

Paul asked, "And when were you first aware of this gentleman's involvement with Howard Hughes?"

"About the time that this picture was taken, and I can date this picture pretty closely."

Paul told him that the Sikorsky had been recently restored to its original condition and that this was a recent photograph.

"Yes, sir, we put some engine controls in it that we transplanted from a Constellation. I remember him when we were doing the engine control work with materials from the Constellation. I held the flashlight for him when he was doing some close work on electronic flight controls. He was

---

[6] Of approximately fifty-three S-43 Sikorskys built, Howard Hughes's Sikorsky is the last example still flying. It was bought by Hughes in 1937—one of only two that were privately owned—for his planned record-breaking flight around the world, but was not used. It was confiscated from Hughes by the U.S. government during WWII to be used by the Coast Guard. Hughes was able to get it back to use for a test aircraft while designing the "Spruce Goose." Howard crashed it into Lake Mead in 1942, killing two of the crewmen. It was retrieved by Navy divers from 200 feet of water. Frank Mann helped Howard Hughes rebuild it at the cost of three million dollars. It was purchased from the Hughes estate in the eighties by California entrepreneur Ron Van Kregten. Hughes's S-43 Sikorsky was restored at Wolfe Air Park, south of Houston, Texas, by antique aircraft restorer Bob Wagstaff.

H. T. Bryer

Standing before Howard Hughes's restored S-43 Sikorsky amphibious aircraft, Houston, 1991. From left to right: Bob Wagstaff (restorer), James Drury, Frank Mann, Bill Bush (Howard Hughes's chief pilot for 34 years), Doug Descant, and Paul Bryer. Photo courtesy Doug Descant.

quite a character. And I remember reading that it was F. C. that was brought in to reconstruct the S-43 when Howard crashed it in Lake Mead in the forties. That was an oddball aircraft, anyway. Sikorsky built aircraft in numerical order and this one is somewhat out of numeric order; it's an S-43, and I'm more familiar with the S-42."

Paul interrupted with, "That's what I wanted to hear. Thank you very much; you've made this interview a success."

Frank Mann gives a thumbs up from the hatch of the S-43 Sikorsky once owned by Howard Hughes.

Paul then asked Mr. Graham if he knew much about the development and building of the 618-foot-long *Glomar Explorer* (USNS *Glomar Explorer* T-AG-193), an ocean-going ship that Howard Hughes developed and had built for the CIA in 1971. The project's classified name was "Project Azorian," though the press often referred to it as "Project Jennifer." This project was deceptively touted to the public as a ship that could mine manganese nodules off the deep ocean floor. But the covert project's real intent was to build a ship-mounted grappling arm that could reach down miles into the ocean and retrieve sections of an armed Russian nuclear submarine that sank in 1968, 1500 miles northwest of Hawaii.

In 1974, the *Glomar* retrieved some sections of the sub, but large pieces of it broke loose from their apparatus and plummeted back down to the bottom of the ocean. Along with the materials brought up were a number of dead Russian submariners who were later reburied at sea.

In conversations with Frank, Paul had heard that he had been called by Hughes to the Edmonds Washington area to help in the design of the *Glomar Explorer's* grappling arm. The grappling arm was developed by the Western Gear Company of Everett Washington just north of Edmonds. So Paul took the opportunity to ask Mr. Graham if he had any knowledge of a Black man being involved in the covert project. Mr. Graham couldn't offer Paul any help on that subject, but he did tell Paul a little story of his own experience with the Jennifer Project.

Mr. Graham was an avid artist. He loved to draw and paint maritime subjects. He bragged about how when he was a younger man he would run around the Houston office with diagrams of the whole *Glomar* project. He was given a photograph of the *Glomar* at a time when the project was "hush hush." He used it to paint an oil on canvas painting of the ship, which he hung on his office wall.

The morning after the announcement on the news of the bringing up of the Russian submarine, he was surprised by a prank played on him by an office coworker.

The Glomar Explorer, *US government photo.*

"That morning, when I came into my office, I was surprised to find that someone had tied a string to a toy submarine and hung it off the frame of my painting of the *Glomar Explorer.*"

Chapter 17
Frank Talk

Besides the few newspaper and magazine articles written about Frank, his sparse paper trail has made it very hard to document his life and accomplishments. Over the years, Paul had interviewed Frank on audio and video tape. Sometimes these informal interviews would take place while they were just sitting around Frank's shop, having a beer. Frank had a lot to say about life in general and more about his own life, in particular.

In a 1987 video interview aired on a local PBS television station, Frank shared some off-the-cuff tips on how to live a full life:

Tip #1, never associate with slow women. "I have had two or three slow women. Now, as far as women go, I don't want to have one that I keep having to put on the brakes for. Now, personally, people get after me about younger women. I'm seventy-nine years old, what do I want with a woman my age? What can she do for me? We couldn't do anything for each other. So, if you get a younger person, they are going to give you young ideas. They are going to keep you stepping, hopping, snatching, grabbing, and trying to hold on. And I'm very happy now that I don't feel any older than twenty-four or twenty-five years old.

"I have had a very beautiful life. I have enjoyed everything in life that I have wanted to do and, at my age today, I am still enjoying life.

"Most people my age are either sitting around or in a wheelchair. They don't walk; they don't do much of anything, nothing for enjoyment. But today, I still feel like I shouldn't let this happen to me, and I am not going to let this happen to me. I think that if and when I die, I'll die on my feet, because I'm not just going to lie down and give up."

Tip #2, to young people, develop a plan for your life and stick to it. "I think every young person should have a viewpoint of what they want to be when they get older. I think that every individual should have a kind of plan for their life, for the simple reason, if you don't plan your life, you won't have a life.

"If someone sees me and wants to be like me, if I can give them any special pointers on life, I will be very happy, too.

"You have to be inspired and want to be somebody if you have any plans for the future. Lots of people today don't care about the future for the simple reason that they are either lazy, alcoholics, on dope, or doing something that isn't contributing to their future at all. If you start out young like this, when you get older what can you say? You can't say anything because you have already wasted half of your life."

Tip#3, make your life an inspiration to others.

"If you are never happy with what you have done in life and you want to do something different, something bigger, better, finer, this helps the human body, it helps the mind, and it helps anybody who is involved with you. Now, another thing that I like about this is that if people see you out on the street and you are getting along fine, and you are doing things and accomplishing things, you also inspire them. And if they want to be around you, encourage them to be more than just another pair of pants and shoes walking down the street."

On personality, Frank had this to say. "A lot of young men don't have a clue about what it takes to have a good personality. A lot of them will just stand around in clubs with scowls or unpleasant looks on their faces. They don't know how to talk to people or feel around to see what the other person would like to talk about." He said, "There are a lot of young men in the clubs that dress better and are a lot better looking than me. Hell, you could put me in a bathtub and skim ugly off of the water for three days. But it is not really the looks of the person, but the way that he talks and carries himself, that attracts the other person."

In another taped interview, Frank shared more of his philosophy. "Now, personally, I say that today I wish more of my people, my race, would get involved in more than just football, basketball, and baseball— these things that they look forward to—because there just isn't enough teams to hire all of the people that want to be involved."

On the subject of his health, Frank said, "Not bragging, but it is true, the average man that has been broken up and been in as many accidents as me, is not walking today. I'm very fortunate and lucky that I'm able to; if I feel like going out there and dancing, I don't bar anyone from the dance floor."

On religion and his relationship with God, Frank was very candid. "I have my own religion. I don't get on my knees every time I feel like praying. I don't [regularly] visit the churches—I go occasionally. But my conception of religion is being to the other fellow what you would like for him to be to you. You do what you think is necessary to be the type of man that God can appreciate. And I say this, I do think God does appreciate me. If he hadn't, would I have been able to do all of the things that I did? Would I still be here? Would I still be feeling good, and still be playing? No. How many more eighty-four-year-old men do you know that are out there on the street at night, playing, having a good time, got young women fighting over him? I'm proud of it, believe you me."

Chapter 18

The First Hospital Stay

I n 1990, Paul was at work several hundred miles away from Houston when he received a call from Frank's shop manager, Mr. A. C. White. "Paul, this is A.C.—I've got some bad news for you. Frank is in the hospital." Paul asked what was wrong with him. A.C. told Paul that Frank had been having nosebleeds, he had passed out, and he had been admitted to a hospital.

Paul rushed back to Houston and when he visited the hospital that evening, he found that Frank had been suffering from malnutrition. When Paul entered Frank's room, he found him a bit tired but in a good mood and joking around with an attractive nurse who was taking his vitals. Paul interrupted and asked Frank, "What happened to you, buddy?"

Frank answered, "I don't know, but these people tell me that I am suffering from malnutrition. But I don't believe them. Hell, I had two Twinkies yesterday."

"Why haven't you been eating, Frank?"

"I don't know, Paul. I just haven't had an appetite."

"Well, I'll have my out-of-town work done soon. When I get back in town, you and I are going to hit some of our old night spots. You had better have you dancing legs back in shape."

"Make you a deal, Paul. You bring me a beer and some of your barbecued brisket, and I'll take you up on it. I'll be out of this joint by tomorrow."

"I bet you will, Frank. But you had better let them fatten you up while you're in here. I'll bring you something good tomorrow."

A sour-faced nurse had been standing in the background. She was listening to their conversation as she feigned reading Frank's chart. With an air of authority, she abruptly moved between Frank and Paul. "Visiting hours are over, sir. It's eight forty five. You'll have to leave right now!" Paul was irked by the nurse's abruptness. For Frank's sake, he ignored his brusque treatment at the nurse's hands.

"See you tomorrow, Frank; behave yourself."

Paul left the room, but stopped just outside the door. As the nurse adjusted Frank's IV bag, she leaned over him and laid down the law. "I have to let you know that this hospital prides itself on its dietary regimen. We frown on visitors bringing food to our patients."

Frank answered her with his typical sense of humor. "Well, dear, I hope you don't frown too much, or your face is liable to get a crack in it." The nurse took Frank's insult to heart.

"Now, that is not the kind of talk that I will tolerate coming from a patient."

Frank answered back saucily. "Well, honey, why don't you try to smile at your patients? Then maybe us patients will be able to tolerate you." The nurse fumed, turned, and bolted out of Frank's room, accidently brushing against Paul, who had been standing beside the doorway all the while. Paul watched her as she rounded a corner and disappeared down the hallway. He stepped back into Frank's room.

"Frank, what was that all about?"

"Beats the hell out of me, Paul."

The next day, Paul brought Frank a bucket of fried chicken and some fruit juice. However, Frank seemed to be slipping. His speech was slurred and he was drowsy.

"Frank, are you all right?"

"I feel weak, Paul, and I just want to sleep."

Frank ate some chicken and he drank some juice, but he still had almost no appetite.

After his meal, Frank closed his eyes and he rapidly fell asleep. Paul sat in Frank's room for an hour or so, hoping that he might wake up and have a little conversation.

Paul felt ill at ease about Frank. He suspected something was just not right. He saw the nurses stop by Frank's door several times and look in, but they did not address him or even look at him. Eventually, Paul left.

During the night, Frank rose and, while trying to walk to the bathroom, he fell, striking his head.

All of Paul's fears and suspicions were realized when he came to the hospital the next morning and found an incoherent Frank strapped to his bed. He had stitches in his head and his tongue was hanging out of his mouth. Paul asked a nurse, "What medications are you giving Frank?" He found out that they had him on Haldol, a strong anti-psychotic drug that is used to quiet schizophrenics. The same drug that some nursing homes still use to help manage elderly patients they deem unruly.

Paul was upset. He grabbed Frank's arms and tried to wake him up. "Frank, Frank, can you hear me?" Frank gave Paul a vacant stare; he tried to talk, but it was all grunts and groans.

The cleaning lady came into the room to empty the wastebaskets. She saw that Paul was upset. She tried to comfort him. "Oh, honey, he'll be all right in a few days. You won't even have to come to the hospital to see him. They're going to be putting him in a nursing home."

But her sharing of inside information with Paul only stoked his anger. "What are you talking about? Who's putting him in a nursing home?"

The cleaning lady answered, "The hospital staff. They told him that it would be for his own good, and that he couldn't take care of himself. He really got mad at them; that's when they gave him the medicine to quiet him down."

Paul couldn't contain his anger any more. He stormed out of the room and looked for the nurse responsible for incapacitating Frank. Paul liked to refer to her as "Nurse Ratched," naming her after the cruel tyrannical nurse in the 1962 novel, *One Flew over the Cuckoo's Nest.*

When Paul found Nurse "Ratched" at her station, calmly having a cup of coffee with one of her cronies, he disrupted their Maxwell House moment. "Why did you people put Frank on Haloperidol?"

"Nurse Ratched" didn't appreciate Paul's tone. "Sir, keep your voice down; this is a hospital."

Paul shouted at her. "I want you to take him off of that drug immediately."

The nurse shot back, "I'd like to know what business it is of yours? Are you a family member?"

"No, I am not, but I know that Haldol is an insane asylum drug that you give to crazy people so that you can easily manage them. And that you are trying to turn a brilliant person into a zombie—and it ain't gonna happen, lady!"

"Nurse Ratched" picked up the telephone and she began to make a call. "If you do not leave right now, I am going to call security on you."

Paul leaned into "Nurse Ratched's" face and he let her have it. "Woman, you can call your damn security and you tell your security to meet me in your damn hospital administrator's office because my sister works there and she is going to have your damn job!" The nurse was speechless; Paul had put her in her place. As she slowly hung the phone up, Paul walked to the hospital administration office.

Paul found our sister, Cindy, at her desk and told her about Frank's predicament. "These goddamn people at this hospital are trying to kill Frank. They have got him on some hypnotic drug and he can't even talk. The last time I saw Frank, he could dance for six straight sets without stopping. Now they have got him so he can't even pick up a tissue to wipe his mouth."

Cindy was concerned. "That's terrible. What can I do to help?"

"Give me a list of the people in charge of this hospital and their telephone numbers."

Paul went back up to Frank's room to check on his condition. To his surprise, he found a handwritten sign taped to Frank's door that read "NO ADMITTANCE—MR. BRYER." Paul clenched his teeth as he ripped the sign from the door and went in to check on Frank. Frank was still incoherent.

Paul spied "Nurse Ratched" at her station. She had been watching him. He walked up to her, ripped her sign to pieces, and then deposited it in her waste basket. He turned to a subordinate nurse. "Could I please use your telephone?"

The nurse looked to her superior for guidance; none came. She turned back to Paul. "Is it a local call?" Paul said, "Lady, it can't get no more local."

"What do you mean by that?"

"I mean, this call is to you and your friend here's boss."

Paul called and got the hospital administrator's secretary on the telephone, and finally the administrator, who gave Paul the run around for several minutes. Paul was getting fed up. But in short order, the administrator had Frank's records, which he was looking over. "I see here now; Mr. Frank Calvin Mann. Now, what is the complaint?"

"Humph! Before Frank was brought in here and drugged, he was ambulatory and he could carry on a conversation with anybody. Now, for what reasons I don't know, your doctors and nurses have turned him into a vegetable and have him strapped in a bed. This is not just any old senile person that you people can drug, put in a nursing home, and rob—and that's the end of that story."

The administrator was perturbed by Paul's outburst. "Now wait just one minute, Mr. Bryer. You're making some strong accusations here. But, if there is any truth to what you are saying, we will get to the bottom of it. I will schedule a conference with all the involved parties. If you want to bring legal representation, you are welcome."

Paul thanked the administrator, gave him his phone number, and waited for his call.

During the meeting, which was held in a hospital conference room several days later, the staff listened to "Nurse Ratched's" complaints about Paul's constantly watching over Frank and interfering with the nurses. She accused Paul of giving Frank beer and drugs. When Paul's turn came, he laid out his case and impressed the staff that his concerns for Frank were genuine. He later arranged for and received power of attorney over Frank's medical treatment. In a twist of irony, the board decreed that the nurse was not allowed in Frank's room unless accompanied by either Paul or another nurse.

When Paul arrived in Frank's room after his victory, he was surprised to find that the hospital had set a table for Frank and his guests, complete with fine china, a 32-inch crystal platter heaped with grapes and all manner of fruit, and numerous elegant pastries. The table remained replenished daily until Frank was discharged.

To combat a proclamation from the nurse that Frank was suffering from dementia, and that he was incapable of handling his own affairs—and to eliminate the possibility of Frank being sent to a nursing home when he was released—Paul requested that Frank be cut back on all of his medication. When Frank was free from the effects of the anti-psychotic drugs, he was tested by an independent psychologist. After Frank's tests, Paul received a copy of the report stating, among other things, that Frank's level of intelligence was on a superior plane of human capability and that he had no dementia. The examiner also thanked the hospital staff for referring this very interesting individual to him.

On the way out of the hospital, Paul escorted Frank as he was being wheeled into an elevator by an attractive nurse. As the elevator door closed, Frank looked up at her and said, "Say, young lady, I can see by looking at you, that you are a person with fine taste. I bet that you like antiques, don't you?"

The nurse smiled at Frank and answered, "Why, yes, I love antiques. In fact, I have a whole apartment full of them."

Frank replied, "Well, why don't you take me home with you then?"

Paul brought Frank home. He fed him well, got him started on nutritional supplements, and promised never again to let this happen to his friend.

Chapter 19

The Last Hospital Stay

I n the latter part of 1992, Frank's health began to fail again. Paul took him to a doctor with the understanding that it was just to be an examination for an esophageal constriction. Paul left Frank at the clinic while he ran some errands. His errands took longer than he planned. When he returned to the clinic, he expected to find Frank frustrated and waiting to give him hell for leaving him waiting so long. However, when he arrived, he looked around the waiting room and Frank was not there. The receptionist saw Paul and spoke to him. "Sir, you are with Mr. Mann, aren't you?"

Paul answered, "Yes, I am."

"Well, the doctor would like to speak with you."

Paul entered the doctor's office and got right to the point. "Is there something wrong with Frank?"

The doctor answered, "Mr. Bryer, Mr. Mann is doing fine. We've admitted him to Herman Hospital to recuperate."

"Recuperate from what? I just brought him in here for an examination!"

"Mr. Mann had laparoscopic surgery performed on his pancreas to remove a golf-ball-sized tumor."

Paul was visibly upset; he reminded the doctor that he had power of attorney over Frank's medical affairs, and that Frank was operated on without his permission.

"Mr. Bryer, I can assure you that Mr. Mann will be fine. We just have to wait for the results of the biopsy. If the results are negative for cancer, then Mr. Mann can go home in a short while."

Paul was upset. He got Frank's documentation and contact information from the receptionist. When Paul got home, he called Frank in his hospital room. He told Frank that he was coming up to see him. Frank told Paul that he was fine and he just wanted to rest and it would be better for Paul to come up in the morning.

Frank with a serious expression on his face, a rare occurrence.

During the night, Frank rose from his hospital bed and groggily walked into the bathroom. As he stood, a hemorrhage from the surgery caused blood to leak from his body, forming a pool on the floor. Frank slipped in the blood, falling and striking his head. Frank was rushed into surgery, where his doctor tried, unsuccessfully, to cauterize his bleeding pancreas.

Paul woke up the next morning with his telephone ringing. It was Frank. "How are you doing, Paul?"

"Fine, Frank, is everything all right?"

"Well, Paul, I got a problem."

"What is it, Frank?"

"Well, they got a Catholic priest praying over me and I'm trying to figure out if I'm going to go up or down."

Frank told Paul about his hemorrhage, his fall in the bathroom, and the doctor's efforts to stem the flow of blood.

"I'm on my way to you, Frank," Paul said, "hold on."

When Paul arrived at the hospital, he met with Frank's doctor in a conference room. "What's wrong with Frank?"

The doctor said, "When we operated on Frank and removed the tumor, we nicked a vein. Though we cauterized it, it opened up and he began to bleed internally."

Paul asked, "How is he doing now?"

The doctor answered, "Not good. I tried my best to go back in there with a laparoscope and cauterize that vein, but it keeps leaking blood."

Paul was physically shaken and deadly serious when he next addressed the doctor. "You had better not let that man in there die. If you do, you will be responsible for the death of one of the greatest Black role models that ever lived."

The doctor was affected greatly by what Paul had just laid upon him. "This is serious, Mr. Bryer. What are you talking about?"

Paul opened his valise and he pulled several large newspaper articles out of it and laid them flat on the table before the doctor. Some of the articles bore Frank's picture and the headlines read, "The Black Engineer Behind Howard Hughes," and "Mr. Mann, Aerospace Engineer, Wins Awards." When the doctor, who happened to be Black, read this material, he understood fully where Paul was coming from and tears welled up in his eyes.

He called a noted thoracic surgeon who opened up Frank's chest cavity and successfully sutured his leaking vein.

Frank rallied, but the loss of blood and the repeated surgeries had taken a toll on him. He was weak and he required an extended recuperation period in the hospital.

Several weeks passed, during which Paul regularly visited Frank in the hospital. Shortly before Paul anticipated that Frank might be ready to leave the hospital and come home, he received a telephone call; it was from Frank's doctor. "Mr. Bryer, we would like to see you at the hospital."

Paul asked, "What for?"

"Mr. Mann has been running a fever and the antibiotics that we had been administering to him aren't working."

Paul was angry. "Why are you calling me now? You should have called me the minute that Frank got the fever!"

When Paul got to the hospital, he met with Frank's doctor and his associates. They filled Paul in. "Mr. Bryer, Frank is septicemic. He has a full-blown blood infection." Paul asked the cause of this infection. The doctor told Paul that it could be caused by any number of things. "These things happen in hospitals." He told Paul that he wanted to enroll Frank in a blind study using a twenty-first century experimental antibiotic. "Half of the patients get the drug and half get the placebo."

Paul agreed to let them enroll Frank in the experiment. "I won't stand in your way; a fifty-fifty chance is better than none at all."

Whether Frank received the new antibiotic or the sugar pill, we'll never know. But whatever it was, it didn't work and Frank's fever continued to rage. Paul comforted Frank in the intensive care unit. He asked Frank a question. "Frank, these people made a mistake and got you into this situation. What would you like me to do? Do you want me to sue them?"

Frank opened his eyes and looked at Paul. "No, Paul. I have lived a long life and I've enjoyed every minute of it. There ain't no need of bringing hardship on these people. They were only trying to help me."

"Okay, Frank, I'll respect your wishes. You're looking a little rough, though, and I know that you don't like these nurses messing with you. So I'm gonna clean you up. How about it?" Frank nodded. Paul took a pan and placed it under Frank's head. He gently shampooed Frank's hair, and then he dried it with a towel.

The Black surgeon, the one who had operated on Frank and accidentally caused his hemorrhage, was standing out of Paul's sight in a curtained area behind them. He watched covertly as Paul dried and combed Frank's hair. Paul put shaving cream on Frank's face and gave him a shave, being very careful not to nick Frank's neat little mustache. Frank was forbidden water, so Paul took a glycerin stick from a cup of ice and soothed Frank's parched lips. At this point, the surgeon stepped up and put his hand on Paul's shoulder. He said, "Paul, when I first met you, I wasn't sure about your motives. I couldn't understand why a person like you could have such a strong interest in a man like Frank. But I have been standing back here and watching how you have been caring for Frank, and I don't think that there are many sons who would do for a father what you did for him. I can see now that you truly love him."

Frank died shortly thereafter and, according to his wishes, he was cremated. Paul oversaw a memorial ceremony for Frank that all of his local friends attended. Local television and newspapers carried the announcement of Frank's death, and the Hollywood trade publication *Variety* carried his obituary.

Frank's final request was that his ashes be sprinkled into the Pacific Ocean from a biplane, from the end of Los Angeles International Airport's runway all the way to Catalina Island.

Paul still has Frank's ashes, and when we accomplish the mission of getting Frank's story told (which, hopefully, this book that you are holding in your hand will do), the last scene of the saga will bring Frank's life full circle—from the time that Frank was a young boy going up to the sky in a biplane with the intention of jumping out and ending his life, to the time his ashes are released into the blue Pacific from another biplane by his friend who loved him and stuck with him until the end.

Life look

1-800 530 8940

CPSIA information can be obtained at www.ICGtesting.com
Printed in the USA
236179LV00001B/27/P

9 780983 258308